MOTHS
MOSQUI

THE WARTIME DIARIES OF
WING COMMANDER H. C. RANDALL D.F.C.

Hal Randall standing in front of a No.616 Squadron
Meteor, 1953.

Edited by
Martin F. Mace

To find out about other titles produced by
Historic Military Press visit our website at
www.historicmilitarypress.com.
Alternatively please write to us free of charge at
Customer Services, Historic Military Press,
Freepost SEA 11014, Pulborough, West Sussex, RH20 4BR,
or telephone our freephone number: 0800 071 7419.

HISTORIC MILITARY PRESS

MOTHS TO MOSQUITOS
The Wartime Diaries of Wing Commander H. C. Randall DFC

First published 2001 by Historic Military Press,
Green Arbor, Rectory Road, Storrington, West Sussex, RH20 4EF.

ISBN 1-901313-06-9

Printed in the United Kingdom by
Selsey Press Ltd., 84 High Street, Selsey, Chichester, PO20 0QH
Telephone: 01243 605234

HISTORIC MILITARY PRESS
Green Arbor, Rectory Road, Storrington, West Sussex, RH20 4EF.
Telephone/Fax: 01903 741941

www.historicmilitarypress.com.

CONTENTS

FOREWORD

by

Group Captain G.D. Sise DSO & Bar, DFC & Bar, Royal Air Force (Retd)

The vital role played by the anti-UBoat squadrons of Coastal Command during World War II is well known. Less has been written about the development of the anti-shipping squadrons of that Command. This book about Wing Commander Randall's wartime experiences goes a long way to filling that gap and few men are better qualified to tell that story.

The author's account of his two tours of operation with anti-shipping squadrons gives an excellent insight into the important role performed by these units from the early years of the war when the Blenheim aircraft was employed on operations for which it was not well suited, to the development of the Strike Wings with their devastating firepower.

His description of the many hazardous operations in which he took part while carrying out reconnaissances in daylight along the coastline of enemy occupied territory and of strikes against heavily defended enemy shipping convoys, is a testimony to the bravery, skill, determination, and devotion to duty of the aircrew of the anti-shipping squadrons. Losses were heavy, but this was an important part of the war effort and the attacks had to be carried out despite the risks involved.

But there was also a lighter side to life in the squadrons. There were brief moments of relaxation and hilarity, particulary after a successful operation had been carried out, which provided a much needed escape from the grim reality of the war. The author's sense of humour shines through in his description of some of these activities.

The passage of time has not diminished my friendship with, and admiration for, Wing Commander Randall and for the aircrew and groundcrew of the anti-shipping squadrons. It is a privilege to have been given the opportunity to write this foreword.

Melbourne, Australia, May 2001

EDITOR'S NOTE

Some years ago, whilst still in my teenage years, I encountered the amazing collection of photographs that Hal Randall had accumulated during his RAF service for the first time. I knew then that I was looking at an important part of Second World War history - one that needed to be recorded for future generations. When, a couple of years later, Hal informed me that he also had a diary that detailed this service, the touch paper that led to this book was lit.

In a sense 'Moths to Mosquitos' is a photo diary. It has not been our intention to provide a definitive summary of Wing Commander H. Randall's wartime career or, for that matter, of the squadrons in which he served. This book has been created to provide the reader with an informative and interesting insight into wartime life in RAF Coastal Command. Sometimes the stories will contain a spark of humour, sometimes sadness. It is hoped that the necessity, starkness and reality of being a wartime Coastal Command pilot will be imparted upon the reader.

For me, born many years after men and women such as Hal brought peace to Europe, it has been a privilege to be given the opportunity to edit his diaries. I hope that, like me, you will enjoy the book, and ponder to remember the debt that the civilised world owes to people like Hal Randall and Bill Sise.

Martin Mace,
Storrington, West Sussex. May 2001

CHAPTER ONE - **TRAINING**

Three Avro 621 Tutors rest on the grass at Cranwell, with others taking off in the background.

CRANWELL

I first arrived at Cranwell in 1937 - one of 32 on my intake. This was, by peacetime standards, a relatively large number. By now the build-up of the armed forces in Great Britain was underway, courtesy of the performance of Adolf Hitler and Nazi Germany. Our working uniform was to be the normal officer tunic with grey flannel trousers (blue trousers were kept for best). We also had the regular peaked cap with a white band or a forage cap with a white panel at the front.

I was put in 'D' flight for the flying training. We flew Avro Tutors, a biplane with an air-cooled radial engine that had two open cockpits in tandem. My first flight was on the 14th September 1937, and after $10^1/_4$ hours dual, I went solo on the 7th October. It wasn't until the second term, however, that we began to practice aerobatics. My school nickname of 'Tubby' had followed me through 'crammer' exams for Cranwell, and stayed with me throughout my service career.

Cranwell from the air, 1937. Note the size of the airfield located behind Cranwell's characteristic main building.

To practice these aerobatics, my instructor had always taken me to a 'T' shaped lake located to the west of Cranwell. He had shown me that by flying down the 'T', the airfield would eventually come into view allowing a safe and easy return to base. On my first solo trip here, I duly turned down the 'T' and began to anticipate the airfield coming into view. When it didn't I belatedly reached for the map and began to sweat! Despite my best efforts at trying to find the airfield, I was eventually forced to admit that I was lost! I continued to fly around, becoming increasingly concerned. Trying to read the map at the same time, I suddenly stumbled upon a previously unseen airfield. I could not see a single aircraft, but there was a lovely long runway. Considering that this was my only option I began my approach.

On landing, I taxied over to some men who were working beside the runway and shouted at them. "Where is this?". Replying, they pointed out the direction of Grantham. A little bit more knowledgeable in respect of my location, I took off and headed back to Cranwell, blissfully unaware that I had just unofficially opened Cottesmore!

PRISONER OF ZENDA

We soon realised that a flight cadet's pay was not much, and as a result our social activities were limited. There was a camp cinema which, whilst cheap, was often great fun. A film with any 'sob stuff' in it inevitably sparked off ribald comments from the airmen! We had a good laugh in the Prisoner of Zenda when the details of the guards were discussed for we had just been practising the setting of guards in our drill lesson.

Cranwell was a big camp and the largest part of it was the wireless school.

The Handley Page Hampden, (originally called the HP52). Shown here is the prototype, K4240.

It was here that airmen were trained to work on and operate the various wireless sets that were in service. There were in fact two airfields - the main one to the south, which we used, and a smaller one on the north side from which large lumbering Vickers Valentia troop carriers operated. These were used as flying classrooms for the trainee wireless operators.

Designated an Army Co-operation aircraft, I first flew solo in a Hawker Audax on the 29th March 1938.

By March 1938 we had converted to Hawker Harts that had been replaced in frontline service by Blenheims and Hampdens. The Harts, powered by water cooled Rolls-Royce engines, were much bigger than the Tutors. On the 29th March I went solo in yet another type - the Audax, which was a variant of the Hart. From now on, we were solo in the Audax, and dual in the Hart, practising aerobatics, spinning, formation flying, instrument flying and cross-country work. We also had to do a height test, which one did solo. This involved climbing to 18,000 ft without oxygen, before being allowed to return to earth again!

In October we witnessed the arrival of the first twin engined trainer, the Airspeed Oxford, at Cranwell. These were new trainers with hydraulically operated flaps and undercarriage. They were thus a large improvement on the older Anson used elsewhere, in which you had to manually wind down the undercarriage and pump down the flaps. The training on these Oxfords consisted of take-off and landing, instrument flying using the new modern instrument panel, and flying on a single engine. Also in October we started our night flying. However, the end was almost in sight, for on the 18th December I was finally awarded my wings or flying badge.

DROGUE

The progress continued, for in January 1939, we were all moved to the Advanced Training Squadron. It was here that we were finally taught to use our aircraft as a weapon. The lessons included quarter attacks - attacking from the side - and stern attacks. The target on these occasions was a drogue towed on a long rope behind one of the RAF's older aircraft, such as a Hart or Audax. The weapon was a camera gun used to provide evidence of one's accuracy - or lack of it. During one quarter attack I managed to loose sight of the drogue behind the Audax's long nose. Cursing I searched hard and whilst trying to relocate the target I flew clean through the towrope. The drogue, suddenly freed from its master, began to drift towards earth. In an effort to redeem myself, I followed the drogue down and pinpointed where it fell. That evening I jumped in my car, found the spot and recovered the errant drogue. Naturally, I had a photo taken of me standing alongside my first kill!

These quarter attack practices were, like the real thing, not without danger. During May 1939 we had a fatal accident, in which both of the pilots were killed. Whilst practising quarter attacks on the drogue, their aircraft collided, sadly falling to earth before anyone was able to escape.

Proudly showing my first kill - the drogue I brought down after I flew an Audax through it's towrope.

In March, I was sent out with one of our Flight Sergeant (F/Sgt) instructors. We flew to Ternhill in an Audax to bring back another aircraft. Arriving just in time for lunch, the F/Sgt instructed me to go to the Officer's mess, whilst he trooped off to the Sgt's mess. At this time Ternhill was being used as a flying training school where they trained short service officers. I hadn't gone far when I was brought to a halt by an irate Flight Lieutenant, who wanted to know what the hell I thought I was doing being improperly dressed. Thankfully I was able to explain that I was from Cranwell, and that the grey flannels I was wearing were our

Running up the 530-hp Rolls Royce Kestrel engine on an Audax at Cranwell. This engine gave the aircraft a top speed of 170mph.

working dress. His reaction was a grunted reply along the lines of "they would do something weird there!" This was not the end of the confusion, for throughout my time in the mess I was the centre of attention - there I was with wings but no rank, whilst they all had Pilot Officers insignia, but no wings!

Squeezing into the cramped rear cockpit of an Audax. If required a .303" Lewis machine gun could be bolted to the attachment just behind the passenger.

SLOW AND LOW

In June 1939 we moved again, this time to Sutton Bridge. Sutton Bridge was a practice camp located on the Wash, from where we could fire live ammunition and drop bombs all within the safety of the ranges. The results of my efforts never lived up to my expectations - especially with the air-to-ground front gun firing. This involved diving onto the target using a ring and bead sight and firing the .303 machine gun through the propellor. We also had to fire guns from the rear tandem cockpits, and this was even more difficult and involved than firing the front gun. The first problem was simply my lack of height! I was unable to depress the gun far enough unless I was standing on the rear-folding seat. Balancing on the seat half in and half out of the cockpit would have been considered a dangerous occupation were it not for the D-ring and strap

Warming up prior to take off. Note the variety of civilian and military types in the background.

on the bottom of the parachute, which was fixed to a hoop on the cockpit floor. Further help with accurate shooting came in the form of your fellow pilots who would do their utmost to fly as slow and as low as possible.

Bombing practice was almost as basic. To bomb, the trainee in the back would lie full length on the floor and pull open a metal shutter allowing a clear view of the ground. Using a bombsight you would direct the pilot via a Gosport tube connected to his helmet, thereby tracking over the target. When the target reached the correct spot on the sight, the bomb would be released. To help achieve this, the pilot had the somewhat unenviable task of flying the plane as steadily as possible, at the correct speed whilst absolutely level! The sheer effort required to be this accurate was compounded by one further fact - the water-cooled engines! The radiator was located just in front of the hole through which the bomb-aimer was looking, and often one would watch as a bead of oil gathered on the bottom of the radiator. It would then choose the most inopportune moment to detach itself, fly back and plant itself on the bomb-aimer's face! This was a small price to pay for the thrill of trying to hit the target.

FURY CRASH

The Hawker Fury was an aircraft type with which I was to have much fun. The Fury was a single seat fighter that had been superseded in front line service by the Gladiator and Hurricane. Once airborne it was a delight to fly. I did encounter one slightly irritating fault - simply getting it off the ground! For a short ass such as myself, the Fury was difficult to taxi, as I could not easily correct any swing on take-off or landing. My short legs couldn't wind the rudder bar far enough back or operate the brake pedals on the rudder bar properly.

Bouwen's Fury after he lost his bet. Having landed on the wrong side of the road, his aircraft bounced, stalled and then buried its nose into the ground.

I wasn't the only person to suffer at the controls of a Fury. I remember that one afternoon several of us were lazily sitting beside a hanger watching aircraft landing over the adjacent road. One of the pilots, Bouwen, bet us that he could land his Fury really close to the road. The bet was on, and he certainly did his best not to lose. He did come in close - too close! He came down so badly that his approach brought him to earth on the other side of the road. Rolling forward he hit the tarmac and his plane was thrown up in the air. The Fury stalled and buried itself nose first in the ground right in front of us!

It was on the 28th July 1939 that these antics came to an end with my departure from Cranwell. Some of the trainees went to fighter units, a few others to flying boats in Coastal Command, whilst the rest, myself included, were allocated to bomber Squadrons.

One of my fellow trainees examines the cockpit of a Hawker Hurricane. This is a Mark I with the Watts two-blade propellor.

WAR

On the 29th July 1939 I was commissioned as a Pilot Officer and allocated the service number 33444. I was given a fortnights leave and then posted to Hemswell, deep in the Lincolnshire countryside. Hemswell was home to my new unit No. 144 Squadron, equipped with Handley Page Hampdens. The Hampden was an odd looking aircraft, having as it did a fuselage shaped like a tadpole!

To get familiar with the airfield and its environs, my flight commander took me up in an old Anson. Following this, I went solo in one of the Hampdens, though once again this was a flight full of surprises. The Hampden was the first aircraft I had flown with such sophisticated engine controls. I found that the engines didn't respond as rapidly as I was expecting. The situation reached its peak on my final approach when I found myself getting lower and lower - slightly worrying when one considers that Hemswell is located on the only ridge of high ground in Lincolnshire! Just as my heartbeat was reaching a peak I managed to rectify things and made a more or less perfect landing. Indeed I went on to do another 10 hours flying before being sent to Manston on a navigation course.

I was at the School of Navigation at Manston in the last days of August 1939. Manston, right in the East of Kent and the nearest military airfield to the continent, was perhaps not the best place to be on a navigation course so close to the outbreak of war. Nevertheless, the lectures naturally proceeded on time and according to the syllabus! This, though, did not last long. On the 2nd September the senior command suddenly broke into a frantic bout of activity. Orders were issued for all the Pilot Officers to commence loading the equipment from the classrooms and accommodation blocks into trucks and railway wagons. The navigation school was on the move to St. Athan in South Wales. It was on the 3rd September that war broke out whilst I was doing an impression of Pickfords somewhere between Kent and South Wales.

St.Athan could hardly have been described as luxurious. We reached new lows in terms of RAF accommodation, having to camp in tents. Thankfully the weather was kind, the only mishap being when one of the tents burnt down. The lectures restarted, though this time so did flying. This was in Ansons, and predominantly took place over the Bristol Channel and Dartmoor. You were a strong person if you landed after these flights not feeling sick. The staff pilots always seemed to insist on flying torturously low! Pouring over charts and taking drifts, using a bombsight, brought water into my mouth on several occasions. This, combined with the hot bumpy conditions meant that I was often fighting to maintain my composure!

Daily Mirror — BRITAIN'S FIRST DAY OF WAR: CHURCHILL IS NEW NAVY CHIEF

By kind permission MGN

SCARECROW FLIGHT

When the course at St. Athan finished on the 8th October we had expected to be returned to our Squadrons, as the course had only been an attachment. However the outbreak of war and the powers that be deemed otherwise. Most of us were transferred to Coastal Patrol Flights, (C.P.F.), which were to be known more aptly as the Scarecrow Patrol Flights. So I made my way to Abbotsinch, southwest of Glasgow, to join No.2 C.P.F.

At this early stage of the war, Abbotsinch was almost on a care and maintenance basis. The C.O. was a Flight Lieutenant who had been called up from the reserve. No. 2 C.P.F. was the only flying unit stationed on the airfield - mind you this was only in theory, as we actually possessed no aircraft. My friend, Ben, became the flight commander purely on the basis that he was two places above me in the Air Force list! We took to

An excellent view of the front of a de Havilland D.H.82 Tiger Moth that we used during the Coastal Patrol Flights. The unofficial badge of No.2 C.P.F. can be seen top.

occupying ourselves by carrying out orderly officer duties such as deciphering signals - a particularly laborious and tedious business.

Soon after my arrival at Abbotsinch I was detailed to a rather unpleasant duty. I was to be the Officer in Charge of a funeral party for an Air Gunner who had recently been killed in a Hudson crash somewhere else in the UK. I started by visiting the parents who lived in one of the suburbs of Glasgow. I was shown into the best room, where the coffin had been placed, and we discussed the details, such as the date and timings. Come the day, and after the firing party had been paraded and the hearse made ready to go, I gave the order to slow march. Off we went with me concentrating hard to produce my best Cranwell taught slow march. On arriving at the coach that was to take us to the cemetery I brought the parade to a halt. I turned, and to my utter horror and embarrassment, I found that I was about 30 yards in front of everyone else. Goodness knows what the elderly Warrant Officer behind me had been up to, and what the people who lined the route must have thought. At the cemetery worse was to come, though thankfully this time it was the turn of the Warrant Officer to suffer an embarrassment. In an effort to position himself, he had misjudged his footing and stepped back into a newly dug grave behind him. Thankfully I did not see his disappearance. Despite the fact I was still suffering from the slow march débâcle, I don't think I would have been able to control myself.

Whilst passing the time we designed our own crest of a scarecrow with wings and the motto "Tempus Fugit, We Don't". No sooner than the artwork was completed, we learnt that we were allocated our first aircraft. The date was the 6th November. Three of us caught the night train from Glasgow to London, from where another train journey took us to the Maintenance Unit at Brize Norton. Walking out onto the tarmac we clapped eyes on our new steeds for the first time.

BOWHILL'S BLUFF

My first flight in a Tiger Moth was not pleasant. The weather at Brize Norton was sunny but extremely windy. Taxiing out onto the runway and turning into the wind was only achieved with the help of some friendly civilians on each wing tip. Once aloft I very quickly began to feel sick - and indeed I was for the first and only time. From here on things simply got worse, for despite our recent navigation course, we soon became lost. I followed the others up a straight and seemingly never ending railway line, feeling miserable and wanting to land anywhere! Suddenly the other two Tiger Moths turned and started to head away from the railway track. Working on the assumption that, if I continued following the railway line then it must eventually lead to some town that I would be able to recognise, I carried on. Thankfully, I was rewarded by the sight of a small airfield, and on closing in I was able to see the name 'Worcester' spelt out in white stones.

Cold, isolated and barren, the west coast of Scotland was not the most ideal location for protracted patrols in the open Tiger Moth!

It looked good to me, and that was all I needed to know. I quickly put down and taxied up to a hanger where I found a single civilian mechanic. He opened the hanger doors, I lifted the tail of the Tiger Moth onto my shoulder, and the aircraft was hauled inside. No sooner had this been completed than the other two arrived and, likewise, put their aircraft inside the hanger. That evening we spent a very enjoyable time in the town, and the following morning continued our flight to Abbotsinch.

On the 14th December I took part in our first anti-submarine patrol. The theory behind these patrols was extremely technical! Carried out at both first and last light, we were to fly our Tiger Moths down the coast to Ailsa Craig. It was hoped that any U-boat which had surfaced to recharge its batteries would, in a moment of panic, mistake our aircraft for a depth charge laden Swordfish, dive and vacate the area of our patrol. It was the papers who later dubbed these flights as 'Ginger Bowhill's Bluff'. He had, as C-in-C of Coastal Command, resorted to such measures as a result of a shortage of operational aircraft at this early stage of the war.

Almost as soon as one of these patrols began, one soon realised that it was a task for which the Tiger Moth was perhaps not the most suitable aircraft! In the small compartment behind the rear cockpit we had to carry a car inner tube. This was our dinghy! I can remember saying that if we ever had any reason to use the inner tube then we would have ended up looking like blue-arsed baboons! Equally, flying at that time of year in an open cockpit off the Scottish coast was a particularly chilling experience. Despite wearing a balaclava under my helmet and a large scarf, I often returned from a Bowhill's Bluff with a frozen jaw!

PARAVANES

During the patrols we would fly a good distance apart in order to cover as wide an area as possible. On one patrol, Sgt. Carter, saw what appeared to be a periscope following a merchant ship. He dived down on it, circled it, and did all he could to draw the attention of the ships crew

One of our C.P.F. Tiger Moths rests between flights at Abbotinch. This airfield, mainly a temporary Fleet Air Arm base, is now home to Glasgow Airport.

to the danger they were in. Eventually the crew twigged, the boat slowed and the periscope closed in. In fact it closed in so far that it was suddenly pulled aboard the merchant ship, where it became apparent that the periscope had in fact been a paravane that was being towed along by the boat with the aim of cutting mine cables! However, the saga continued.

His heroics meant that Sgt. Carter was now low on fuel, causing him to make a forced landing in a field on his way home. Needless to say we had quite a party that night to celebrate Sgt. 'Paravane' Carter's exploits! Next day I went back to the field with a small maintenance crew who refuelled the Tiger Moth from tins. I then flew it back, though only just clearing some telephone wires that ran along the up-wind boundary of the field.

One evening we had a huge signal, all in cypher which came in for us on the teleprinter. It was all about a large Atlantic convoy that was coming into the Clyde. Naval escorts and long range aircraft patrols were detailed and, right at the end, it was ordered that No. 2 C.P.F. was to be on patrol at Ailsa Craig. As a result three of us flew down to Prestwick, refuelled and then went on to our patrol stations. We flew back and forth past Ailsa Craig, getting colder and colder until lack of fuel forced us to stand down.

We had seen nothing! As we passed up the Clyde approaches we saw the last of the convoy dropping anchor - it had been hours early. This was the first time that I learnt that convoys were seldom where they were supposed to be!

My last flight in a Tiger Moth was on the 30th December 1939. It was a dawn patrol in pretty awful weather, though this time we did get to see the convoy. I do remember an even worse fog - one so bad that I could only find my way back to my hut, whilst driving my car, by shining a torch light out of the side and watching the kerb moving by!

A rather outdated cockpit. Note the ring and bead gun sight pushed back up in front of the pilot.

MEASLES MANSION

Changes were coming thick and fast. On the 15th January I was posted yet again - this time to Bircham Newton in north-west Norfolk. I was to be a navigator in the airfield's Operations Room. On arrival I found one of my Cranwell colleagues doing exactly the same. Our role was to work out and plot the course of the various naval and merchant convoys currently at sea. This would then provide the escorting aircraft with the information they needed to find and shadow the ships. This was, however, not quite the posting we had both wanted - we would have preferred an operational squadron posting.

Soon after my arrival I went down with the measles, along with several others. We were moved into one of the married quarters, which soon became known as 'measles mansion'! When the worst was over and we were allowed out by the MO several of us used to tour round the boundary of the airfield and with various firearms would try and get a rabbit or two for the pot.

Bircham had been a peacetime station and as a result the accommodation was of a good standard. The airfield was already busy. There was an Anson Squadron, No. 206, and 42 Squadron (a torpedo bomber unit) who were still equipped with old Vildebeest biplanes. A new arrival was 254 Squadron who were flying the first of the new Coastal Command long range fighters - the Blenheim - though were not yet fully operational.

A wartime Mark I Hurricane stands watch over a Percival Proctor. This aircraft, a radio trainer and communications type, carries no military markings. This indicates that the aircraft was still on the civilian register or newly requisitioned.

254 SQUADRON

We never lost our urge to get operational, and eventually we succeeded. We finally escaped the Ops. Room as a result of a shortage of navigators in 254 Squadron - joining them on the 1st April 1940. We had Blenheim I's and IV's - both marks being fitted with a pod of four .303 Browning machine guns under the belly, with the ammunition storage in the bomb bay. The Blenheim had been developed as a bomber for Lord Rothermere who had paid for the original prototype. Designed as a bomber it lacked any armour plating in front - except for some behind the pilot and navigator! When some armour was retrospectively fitted it was found that

the Blenheim had become too heavy to remain airborne on a single engine. The W/T set was operated by the Wireless Operator (W/Op) and was of a rather dated design. At the best of times it was difficult to operate and the small number of Corporals trained in its operation soon became in great demand.

My first trip as a navigator, with Sgt. Rees as pilot, was on the 4th of April. It was in a Blenheim 1 - an unfortunate fact, as the Mark 1 was the short nosed version and extremely cramped for the navigator. You sat beside the pilot and would balance the board, with your charts, on your knees. Fighting your way down to the bombsight to take a drift was a real struggle. The longer nosed Mark 4 was thankfully equipped with a table in the nose specially for us navigators! Following my first flight in the Mark 1, I did two more trips as navigator on coastal protection duties and a third checking the four light ships in the area (one had recently been attacked by the Luftwaffe).

As time passed I was also given dual flight training on the Blenheim 1 - these being the only variant that could be fitted out as trainers. On the 8th I went solo. To get practice, I took a number of wireless operators up to get practice on their sets. The 20th saw my first reasonable operational trip - a brief sweep up the Dutch coast looking for German shipping.

SCANDINAVIAN SORTIE

The war was moving fast, and my operational duties were about to catch up. On the 9th April 1940 German forces invaded Norway. They did so in an effort to safeguard their access to supplies of Swedish iron ore. In response an allied expeditionary force went ashore in

Northern Norway on the 15th. On the 23rd I was officially posted to No. 254 Squadron and immediately left with them for Hatston, a Royal Naval air station, in the Orkneys. We were to provide long range fighter support to our embattled troops in Norway by hopefully intercepting the enemy bombers as they flew north.

The enemy - just visible ahead as spot in the sky.

On the 29th April I flew as number 2 to my flight commander in our first attack over Norway. We had been tasked to attack a number of oil tanks, one of which we found already burning. On the 1st May our CO led three of us on another attack. We took off at 0400hrs and commenced a patrol of one of the fjords. An hour into the patrol someone with a keen eye spotted a plane across our path, though somewhat distant. Then the penny dropped. It was a German He-111 bomber. We needed no second bidding, the chase was on!

THE CHASE

To get full power the pilot opened up the throttles fully and then pulled a lever which gave maximum boost to the engines. However things were not quite that simple as the engine needed 100-octane fuel to run with this boost. At that time we were short of 100-octane, so we had been flying on the larger inner fuel tanks, leaving the 100-octane fuel stored in the smaller outer fuel tanks. Therefore to get the boost

Despite our best efforts, and a chase north up Norway, the German failed to be caught.

we needed, if we were to have any chance of catching the He-111, we had to reach across the cockpit and rotate the two large spoked wheels. These wheels, renowned for their ability to catch your fingers, switched the fuel supply from the inner to outer tanks - or visa versa. Suitably supplied, the engines were run at maximum boost - so much so that we were eventually able to catch up with the Heinkel. However, the German crew declined to provide us with an easy target.

The German pilot dived for the ground, swooping down the slopes of the nearest fjord. The CO and I followed pouring all our front gun ammunition after the German. Despite our best efforts we had no effect. Worse still, the German rear gunner was able to get some shots in at my aircraft before sliding away at low level!

MORE NORWAY

Following the excitement of the chase, we carried out further Norwegian sorties, which were interspersed with convoy escort work and practice dive-bombing. One of the latter almost ended in a rather serious situation. During the peak of the dive there was a horrendous tearing noise. The rear hatch of the Blenheim had blown out and attempted to bed itself in the tail plane. Thankfully the damage was not bad enough to impede our landing.

One of No.254 Squadron's Mark IV Blenheims tears along at low level whilst keeping in formation with my aircraft.

On the 9th May, 8 Blackburn Skuas from one of the Fleet Air Arm Squadrons, escorted by six of our Blenheims, were tasked to bomb German shipping in Bergen harbour. It was not a good day, for one of our planes succumbed to the anti-aircraft defences and was shot down. More trouble was to come on the way home.

The ever present snow capped mountainous landscape that so characterised the Norwegian patrols.

Desperately short of fuel, six of the Skuas were forced to land at Sumburgh, before returning to Hatston. One of these was to do what we called a 'wheeler'. The Skua was an ugly aircraft and was renowned for being nose heavy. The heavy weight of the nose meant that as the plane slowed on landing the elevators lost effectiveness, and one of the Skuas on this occasion lost grip, tipped forward and ended up sliding down the runway resting on its nose!

TUSSLE OVER HOLLAND

On the 10th May, four of us, myself included, were sent back to Bircham on a detachment. We had heard that the Germans had decided to invade the rest of Europe and were now pouring into Luxembourg and Belgium. No sooner had we arrived, when three of us were ordered to take our Blenheims on a patrol along the Dutch coast in an effort to harass any German shipping we might find. This mission was uneventful, though it might well have been different for we saw a lot of enemy aircraft in land.

The next day, on the 12th, the same three were again sent back to Holland, this time to act as an escort for British Naval vessels in the Dutch port of Flushing. This was to prove a far more eventful trip. Arriving over the port, the three of us located the British vessels and began circling the

This amazing photograph was taken during an escort patrol for British Naval vessels in the Dutch port of Flushing. We arrived in the middle of a German air-raid - the explosions that can be seen on the ground are their work.

harbour. As I kept watch I suddenly noticed that bombs were exploding in the town centre. Scouring the surrounding skies I found the reason why - there was a mixed gaggle of some seventeen Heinkel He-111s and Junkers Ju-88s that had dived through a cloud layer and were intent on raining their deadly cargo on the town.

Frantic activity broke out in our planes - the tanks were switched over, levers pulled and full boost applied. Once again the chase was on. I attacked a group of four bombers that had been nearest me. Three were either too fast, had managed to break away or escaped into the cloud layer. The fourth, not so lucky German, was a Junkers Ju-88. In the chase I used up all my front gun ammunition on him to, seemingly, no avail. Refusing to give up I found to my surprise that we were faster - so much so that we quickly came up on his starboard side. Formating on him, my crew unleashed the contents of five magazines from the K gun at him. One of the other Blenheims then joined in the hunt, coming at the German from behind - also using up all his front gun ammunition. By this time and being fully aware of our unfriendly intentions, the German pilot was doing everything possible to escape. He opened up, and left us frustrated. Somewhat dejected, the three of us set course back to Bircham.

On landing, my ground crew found two bullet holes in a propeller and two more in one of the wings. The following day the plane was still u/s, and as a result I missed some more excitement. Two of the 254 Squadron Blenheims, along with two from No. 248 Squadron, had gone back to Holland and run into a gaggle of six Me-110s. One of our pilots, Sgt. Tubbs, finally claimed a victory when one of the 110s was brought down by him.

On the 14th May two of us from No. 254 Squadron were detailed to join two aircraft from No. 248 Squadron on another foray across the Channel to Holland. We hadn't been long into the flight when the second of our planes was forced to turn back. Ever since take-off Derek had been unable to prevent one of his engines from repeatedly cutting out. Undeterred, the rest of us ploughed on! However, my turn at non-serviceability came next - exactly as we hit the Dutch coast. Our guns were tested, at which point we found that not one would operate. So I had to abort the mission and turn for home, leaving the two 248 planes to go it alone.

Blenheim Mark IVs in line abreast. This provides the reader with an excellent view of one of the 905hp Bristol Mercury radial engines that powered the Blenheim Mark IV.

No sooner had I pointed the plane northwards when the shout went up - enemy aircraft sighted. Some Me-110s had decided to take an unhealthy interest in our presence, a pretty unpleasant situation when one was totally unarmed! Yet again the cockpit broke into life, and the by now very familiar wheels and levers were spun, yanked and pulled. At full boost we did the only honourable thing and beat it! We must have had a good headstart, for as we raced home across the cold waters of the North Sea, my wireless operator called up and informed us that the Germans had thrown in the towel and given up the chase.

TORPEDO BOATS

Following this raid there then followed a period of inactivity - though I cannot remember why. The weather had been good, as I had done some sunbathing. In fact some days I was on standby all day - all without a whisper of action. On the 19th I heard that Bouwen, who had famously bent a Fury whilst at Cranwell, was reported as missing in action.

The inactivity came to an end on the 21st when three of us were detailed to another recce along the Dutch coast. Once again Derek was forced back with engine trouble. Further on, we entered some thick cloud and myself and the sole remaining Blenheim lost each other! We decided to continue on, finally reaching the Dutch coast unscathed. Ambling along, and trying

Taken from an Avro Anson during my navigation course this sailing boat is in the Bristol Channel..

Crossing the Dutch coast. I took this picture through the side windows of a Blenheim cockpit. In front of me on the stalk is the airspeed indicator.

to avoid the attentions of any more Me-110s, we stumbled across six German torpedo boats close inshore. I asked my W/Op to send a message relaying the details of this sighting. After a few minutes he announced, somewhat irate, that he had been unable to get through. Were any of these Dutch missions ever going to pass off without a hitch? Following a discussion, and the fact that there had been nothing else of interest seen, we decided that the only thing to do was open up a bit and get back to Bircham with the tidings.

LIVING IN BOXES

On the 25th May 1940, I was posted to the most northern airfield at which I was to ever be based - Sumburgh in the Shetland Islands. As well as my most northern posting, it also marked a new low in standards of accommodation. No. 254 was the first Squadron to have been posted here, though there had already been a flight of Gladiators intended for the Island's own defence. The runways had only just been finished, though the same could not have been said about some of the buildings. In fact we were to sleep under canvas!

The mess was a large marquee, and the bar was constructed from empty wooden boxes, each of which had previously been used to transport two 4-gallon petrol canisters. These petrol canisters were the only source of fuel for our Blenheims and, worse still, was the fact that the planes had to be completely refuelled by hand! Initially the fuel also had to be filtered through chamois leather to remove excess water. The boxes soon became the principal, and sometimes only, source of furnishing on the airfield. They were used in the tents as bedside cabinets, chairs and other useful things.

Cold, desolate and windy. That was often what the weather at Sumburgh had to provide. Opened in 1936, this temporary Coastal Command airfield was basic by almost everyone's standards!

BATHS AND SPLINTERS

Bathing and washing at Sumburgh had to rank as the most basic act of all. If one was lucky you might have been given permission to go to the Sumburgh Head Hotel. Here one could avail oneself of fitted bathrooms and running hot and cold water. The only other option available was to bath the Sumburgh way - in an open-air bathtub. This, I can assure you,

Bathing the Sumburgh way.

is no mean task when one bears in mind the northern locality of the Shetland Islands. First of all an old, round wooden bath 'barrel' had to be located. This was then rolled round the airfield to your tent and set up in its entrance. Water was then brought in buckets from the kitchens - cooling nicely as you went. Once set up there was one further risk with these baths - getting splinters in awkward places!

27

As you could imagine, washing soon became a topic of much conversation during our time here. We would dream of the bathroom at the Hotel. The bathroom had a loo that had a rod with a spade handle at the side that you would pull to flush the toilet. One day four of us made the trip to the hotel. One of us, Mackenzie, used the lavatory, only to emerge with a large frown on his face. The rest of us fell about laughing, for we knew only too well

Shaving and washing the Sumburgh way.

what was going through his mind. The day before he had pulled up the undercarriage on his plane after landing instead of the flaps, his aircraft collapsing onto its belly. The undercarriage lever on the Blenheim had a spade grip identical to the toilet flush in the Hotel!

SUMBURGH

As an airfield Sumburgh was not ideal. At one end of the runway you had Sumburgh Head itself, and at the other you would approach over the village itself down a slope. The short runway had the sea at both ends. Although we were there in the summer and the sea was so close, no one swam as the water was far from warm. I have to admit to attempting a paddle once, but this was very rapidly given up as a bad idea! There also seemed to be a perpetual wind at Sumburgh. You were always aware of the sound of empty petrol tins being blown round the airfield. Later, when the Nissan huts finally arrived, sheets of airborne corrugated iron replaced the petrol canisters!

Since moving to the Shetlands the Squadron had been carrying out reconnaissance missions along the Norwegian coast, as well as providing long range fighter cover to our troops in the north of Norway.

At first we had only been meeting German bombers, but as time passed

Looking out over the Pool of Virkie (above) we rest by the sandbagged trenches that were the airfield defences - along with a few of the .303 rifles on show here! Snow and isolation (below) are two of my over-riding memories of Sumburgh.

and the Luftwaffe became more established the risk of an enemy fighter became much greater. A request by our CO for us to operate over Norway only under the cover of cloud was declined by 19 Group, and as a direct result our casualty rate began to climb. Also at this time, on the 28th May, rumours started up saying that the German army was massing in Norway in preparation for an invasion. We were therefore all given a personal issue .303 rifle.

Hardly conversant with such pieces of hardware, we practised by shooting at shags and cormorants flying low over the sea - though thankfully our success rate was worse than terrible. There was also a new issue that began to dominate our conversation - would the Squadron be able to get its planes to Iceland should the Germans invade!

On the 31st of May the final batches of our groundcrew and their equipment arrived in a Harrow. They had made part of the flight from Bircham in an old (with the emphasis on old) Imperial Airways Hercules.

This was a four-engined biplane, and was so old that when the loading had been completed its crew found that they could not shut the rear door!

The pilot, in a fit of inspiration, started up the top two engines and ran them to full rev's - or as close as he dared. This removed the sag in the fuselage, allowing the crew to close the door.

Four Blenheims formating alongside my aircraft provide the ideal opportunity for a piece of air-to-air photography. The letters 'QY' on the nearest aircraft indicates No.254 Squadron.

Throughout June we carried out further recces along the Norwegian coast. We had divided the coastline into sections. 'Stab' was the area from Stavanger to Bergen; 'Bert' was from Bergen to Stadlandet; whilst 'Trost' reached from Stadlandet to Trondheim. In fact, Trondheim was as far north as we could go. On the 3rd June I led three aircraft on a patrol of 'Stab' - one which was to prove quite eventful. First of all we chased a German plane up Hardanger Fjord but despite the by now regular 'boost routine' we failed to catch it. Next we targeted a wireless transmission station on one of the islands, before spotting what appeared to be a German cruiser lying in one of the Fjords!

At this point, things suddenly decided to heat up. Needless to say we did not linger long, repeatedly thanking God for the presence of some very thick cloud. Somewhat upset by our appearance the cruiser opened up with some quite heavy anti-aircraft fire. The fact that this stopped abruptly heralded the arrival of a more pressing problem - three Me-110s on a mission with our name on it! Still being highly gracious we escaped into the cloud and lost them. Returning to Sumburgh and so worn out by all the excitement I crawled straight into my tent to the welcoming relief of my bed. Hardly having had time to close my eyes I was abruptly woken and dragged from under the blankets. I was hustled into the Operations Room and had to answer hundreds of quizzical questions from Group about the mysterious Cruiser we had stumbled upon earlier.

FIGHTER STANDBY

By the 4th June, our Norwegian patrols were becoming more frequent. On this day, one of the patrols had some success. Straddling the coast they had come across a lone Dornier flying boat and, unlike my previous efforts had closed in and made a successful interception.

An image that was to become famous during the Battle of Britain - aircrew on fighter standby. (This was the crew room at Carew Cheriton, taken late in the war).

Three days later it was again my turn to lead a patrol. I remember two things about this flight - firstly that we stuck to 11,000 ft throughout and secondly that I was, for some reason, distinctly nervous. It was important, for everyone's sake, that all of the crew remained alert and kept a very good look out. I would often ensure that the W/Op was in the top turret, as they might have gone down to receive or send a message and been tempted to remain in the relative comfort of the cabin. On this flight I had a W/Op who was adept at taking his time in returning to his turret, and sure enough when I looked back he was not in situ. I indicated to my Navigator to hold tight and pushed the control column forward. This had the desired effect. As the plane tipped forward, the W/Op suddenly appeared in the turret, his face pressed hard against the glass of the dome!

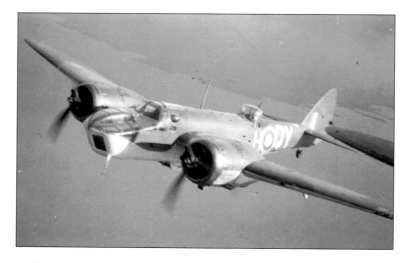

A 3/4 view of a Blenheim Mark IV. By the time production ceased in 1942/1943, some 1,930 Mark IVs had been manufactured. The type saw service in all theatres of war.

As well as the patrols, we were also doing fighter standby at Sumburgh. Both the planes and the standby crews were located at the far end of the runway, our only luxury being a small wooden hut in which we were allowed to rest at night.

To help spread the workload, the Gladiators had remained on the airfield and were also doing the standby duties.

On the same day that I had rudely interrupted my W/Op, I was allocated to the standby flight. During the night an air raid had developed over the

Fair Isle, and four of the Blenheims, supported by all the Gladiators, took off into the dark night sky. They were directed by the radar station located on the northern island of Unst in the general direction of the attackers.

Unfortunately they had very limited control facilities, and this combined with the darkness meant that they never did find the German aircraft.

THE SCHARNHORST

Sergeant Foster, my navigator, sits in the co-pilots seat of a Blenheim. This is a good illustration of some of the flight clothing and insignia that we wore.

On the 11th June, and with myself leading two others, we took off for a recce in the Trondheim area. With the sky cloudless, we approached the fjord at 13,000ft and then we saw her. Filling the fjord, and flanked by a brace of cruisers, was a big German battleship, which we found out later was the Scharnhorst. Following a couple of brief passes we turned and headed for home in an effort to prevent the situation turning nasty.

To plot our course home, the navigators really needed to be able to take drifts on the 'white horses' at sea, or get the direction of the low-level wind from the sea-lanes. These are marks caused on the water by the wind. As we returned home, none of the crew on any of the aircraft managed to get a bearing. As our estimated time of arrival passed, we still had yet to see any sign of land! Coming from Trondheim, we approached the Shetlands from the N.N.E. As they run in a narrow line north to south they presented a rather small target. Beginning to sweat, I decided to carry on, hoping to see, if not the Shetlands, the Orkneys or even further on the north coast of the Scottish mainland. After six hours I came to the conclusion that whilst we were somewhat lost, we must be south of Wick (the airfield on the north east tip of Scotland), and so we turned west. As we began to consume the last fumes in the fuel tanks we spotted land, making our landfall at Kinairds Head. After some 6hours 50minutes we finally landed at Lossiemouth. So relieved was I that I very nearly bent down and kissed the tarmac!

BASIC NEEDS

This had been a particularly gruelling flight, with the time spent in the air normally a more reasonable 4.5 to 5.5 hours. That is, however, still quite long enough to get a very sore bottom as the pilot was strapped in with very limited movement. I can hear you saying, "how did he go all that time without having to spend a penny". The truth is that whenever possible I didn't. The simple act of relieving oneself whilst stuck at 13,000ft in a Blenheim was no easy task. For this purpose we were

provided with two rubber hot water bottle shaped devices, each fitted with a metal cup on the top. One was found up front, and was for the use of the pilot and navigator, whilst the second, in the back, was for the W/Op. Try using one of these in a moving aircraft whilst strapped in and wearing flying overalls! Worse, in cold weather the necessary appendage might be rather on the short side! As a result I got in the habit of standing by the tail

My old friend Parvin, navigating in an Anson on a coastal patrol flight.

before take off, desperately trying to squeeze out every last drop, (thankfully we did not have any WAAF groundcrew).

The presence of the ships at Trondheim made Group send up four Beauforts of 42 Squadron. Late on the 12th they took off escorted by five of our Blenheims. They all got back safely early in the morning of the 13th with the last plane landing after some 7.5 hours. One of the Beauforts had damaged aileron controls and crashed into the sea narrowly missing our tents. The crew, thankfully, were all able to get out.

The 'Scharnhorst' had yet to disappear from the target sheets. On the 16th the CO led three of us as an escort to a mixed force of 6 Hudsons and 3 Beauforts on a raid to Trondheim. The weather let us down. There was a weather front over the North Sea, and although we climbed to

A No.254 Squadron waits in the snow - above. Note how, in an attempt at maintaining operational readiness, the snow has been repeatedly cleared from the taxiways. Below - Airborne again.

23,000ft, we could not get over it. Whilst this flight was remarkable in that it was the first time that I had used oxygen, it was less striking as I lost the rest of the flight in the thick cloud. We eventually struggled back to base only to find that most of the others had already returned.

Another attempt was made the following day, though I was not one of the escorting Blenheims. The attack took the same format as the previous day, and before long the aircraft were returning to Sumburgh defeated by the bad weather. As a result, there were a lot of relieved aircrew in the mess that night - so much so that a party soon developed. The beer had been flowing for some time when a signal came through ordering the Hudson and Beaufort Squadrons to return to their home stations - immediately! I remember one of the Hudson pilots, a Canadian, standing in the entrance to the mess 'marquee' swaying from side to side. With some conviction he solemnly announced that he was going to 'beat the shit out of Sumburgh'. Once airborne, he did exactly this. In fact one of his passes over the airfield was so low that bottles crashed down from the shelves behind the bar.

INJURED

During the night of the 20th I led two others on a routine patrol over the North Sea. As we were rumbling along I suddenly spotted a submarine on the surface. Unfortunately it must have had a keen lookout, for it immediately began to dive. Shouting at my crew I slammed forward the throttle and swung the plane down towards the submarine. It was a race, with us trying to reach him before he disappeared completely. Just as he vanished from sight we raced over the spot where he had been and I released our bombs. The bombs exploded, though they were only 20lb H.E. and 24lb incendiary bombs, so I don't know what happened to the submarine. Forming back up with the others, we continued onwards towards the Norwegian coast, though one of the planes was forced to turn back with engine trouble.

As we hit the Norwegian coast, we soon spotted our next target. A Heinkel He-115 floatplane was lumbering its way north seemingly oblivious to our

Blenheim IVs peel away from formation and bank over towards the British Countryside below.

presence. This time I was determined to make a better job than I had done with the submarine. I guided my Blenhiem with care, deciding to attack the Heinkel from the rear, closing in from slightly below it. As I got within range I opened fire. I went round and attacked a second time, and on this attempt I saw one of the floats on fire. Determined not to give up, we went around for a third attempt. Once again I opted to come in astern and slightly lower, believing that this would be an area where his rear gunner would not be able to see us. I was to be proved wrong.

As we were just in range I opened fire when I felt a hard bang on my right leg. I realised that I had been shot.

Through the hard way I had learnt that this was not the Heinkel rear gunner's blind spot. Whilst I was trying to sort myself out, the remaining Blenheim went around for his third attempt. This time the Heinkel ended up in the cold water of the North Sea, so I suppose we could claim half a kill each. With the Heinkel finished off, I asked my navigator, Sgt Craig, for a course to steer home. Once we were on our way, Craig made a tourniquet out of my tie and one of his pencils in an attempt to stop the bleeding. Luckily he couldn't have been a good first-aider, for in all the confusion he had totally forgotten to later release the pressure on the tourniquet!

Back at Sumburgh, and despite my injuries, we decided to celebrate our 'kill' by beating up the runway. We duly charged up the airfield barely feet from the ground with the throttles wide open! However, we had spoken too soon, as the crisis was not yet over. Having touched down, and with the end of the runway fast approaching, I found that I was

having trouble braking. My injured leg meant that I was unable to operate the rudder bar properly. The Blenheim was an easy aircraft to fly - you could fly round and round a convoy for ages with your feet off the rudder bar and just using the ailerons to turn.

This picture of one of my fellow patients, Tom Beale, was taken from my bed during my time in the Gilbert Bain Hospital. (Is there nowhere that I didn't take my camera?!)

I was taken to the Gilbert Bain Hospital by ambulance, and during the journey I insisted that the bell be rung at least once. I was the hospital's first war wounded and was treated like royalty. The surgeon had me moved to the female ward - my pleasure diminishing when I realised that this was simply because it was the only place where they had room for the x-ray equipment. I was given a spinal injection, which resulted in the weirdest sensations. The surgeon, in an effort to remove the embedded bullet shrapnel, would be moving my leg all about, throughout which it felt to me as if my leg was still resting on the table!

It was from one of my subsequent visitors that I learnt how lucky I had actually been. The Flight Sergeant of 'A' flight had lined up the one and only bullet hole in my aircraft. This sole bullet had entered the nose of my Blenheim before hitting a screw in the navigator's table. This screw had in turn deflected the bullet down through my leg before the rest of it passed out of the bottom of the aircraft. Had it not been for the screw head, then the bullet would have hit me in the lower part of my stomach!

I have one other memory of my time in the hospital. There had been an elderly shepherd brought into the ward, and the rest of us were convinced that he was smoking sheep droppings in his pipe, as the smell was absolutely appalling!

DYCE

Whilst on sick leave at home, the Squadron had been moved to a new home - Dyce. This was to enable the crews to have some rest as well as train our new arrivals. Amongst these new postings were our Squadron's first coloured troops, as we rudely called them. They were Dick Poynter and Bill Sise - both New Zealanders. Bill started somewhat inauspiciously as he bent a Blenheim on his first landing. Our Flight Commander, Bill Bain, had gone up with him in a Mark IV to check him out. After a successful flight, Bill came in too low on his landing. He clipped the boundary wall writing off his undercarriage! His only option was a belly landing.

At the controls of a Blenheim, providing another detailed view of an RAF pilot's flight equipment at this stage of the war.

During the execution of this Bill Bain somehow received a cut on his bottom! Once the aircraft was halted, Bill Bain was rushed to the station sick quarters in an ambulance. I followed behind in the CO's car with Bill Sise. He was extremely worried about Bill Bain, and through the whole journey I had to keep making soothing noises to cheer him up!

THE STAIRS

Injuries not resulting from enemy action seemed to be the order of the day. Soon after the crash landing another of the Squadron became a

In this view of a Mark IV one can see a modification to our Coastal Command Blenheims - four forward-firing machine guns mounted in a pod underneath the cockpit.

victim. It was early one morning when Ken Illingworth hobbled into the flight office looking as if every muscle and joint ached. He had returned from leave the night before and to welcome him back, we had taken him round Aberdeen's various hostelries. Consequently, he was returned to his billet somewhat worse for wear and extremely unsteady on his feet! His bedroom was at the top of a particularly steep flight of steps. In the dark and not wanting to disturb his landlady, he set about climbing his way up. Keeping a tight grip on the one and only banister he made slow but sure progress, almost reaching the top step. At the top his hand went on past the end of the banister and he tipped backwards, crashing back down to the bottom of the stairs. We all firmly believed that it was his inebriated state that had prevented him from breaking any bones.

Much of our time at Dyce was spent on coastal convoy patrol work. One such patrol, though, nearly ended with dire consequences. On this particular patrol our Squadron had sent a single aircraft, flown by Sgt. Tubbs, which was tasked to provide close escort to the convoy. Fighter Control then picked up a plot of an enemy aircraft heading straight for the ships. They scrambled some Spitfires from an airfield further south down the coast and informed Tubbs that help was on its way. As all the groups

Whilst on Convoy patrol work we often encountered flights of Fighter Command Spitfires. This is a pre-war photograph that I had taken, showing a Mark I example.

closed in, Fighter Control may well have become confused over which plot related to which aircraft. Crossing over the convoy one of the Spitfires opened fire on his target. Instantly the radio channel was filled by the indignant protests of Sgt. Tubbs as his aircraft came under fire. The fighters, now realising their mistake, peeled away. Tubbs was thankfully uninjured, and was able to successfully ditch into the North Sea. Both he and his crew were then picked up by one of the ships from the convoy. Worse, thanks to this botched mêlée, the German aircraft had made good his escape and scuttled back towards Norway!

By the time Tubbs had been reunited with the Squadron he was absolutely livid. It was with much difficulty that he was persuaded from going down the coast to 'knock the block' off the Spitfire pilot, who would undoubtedly have come off worse, for Tubbs had been the welter weight champion of the RAF!

CONDORS

On the 6th January 1941 we returned from our rest back to Sumburgh, and the old routine of reconnaissance along the Norwegian coast. Just as bad was the fact that we were back to sleeping in the Nissen huts with their single, and inadequate, stove for heating. And we still had only the wooden crates for furniture!

Another pre-war picture of a Fighter Command type, though in this case a Mark I Hurricane. Note the rows of machine guns in the leading edge of each wing.

The situation had changed little during our absence. Losses on the Norwegian patrols had become too high and the powers-that-be had decreed that for the flights to go ahead we must have cloud cover. It was the losses that we sustained during the summer, as well as those of No. 248 Squadron who followed us, that forced this decision. As a result the number of Norwegian sorties with which we were tasked began to dwindle. Our secondary role was still the defence of the islands, though this still remained largely the responsibility of a flight of Hurricanes that now adorned the airfield.

The Battle of the Atlantic was of increasing importance, and the Germans were using four-engined Focke-Wolf 'Condors' to search for our convoys in the Atlantic. Flying from their Norwegian bases these aircraft could stay airborne for long periods, directing the U-boat packs the whole time. The radar station on Unst could track these aircraft, but could not normally direct us to them, as the range of our radios was too limited. Instead, we had resorted to patrolling across their routes in the hope that we might 'bump' into them!

It was on the 1st May that I led a two aircraft patrol on one of these 'trawling' patrols. Flying north from Unst we encountered a pretty thick layer of cloud at 2,000ft. I guessed that any roving Condor would be keeping low in an effort to avoid the Unst radar station. I decided to go even lower and began the patrol by flying right on the deck. Moments later, and to our utter surprise, we stumbled across a Condor. The German aircraft was just below the cloud deck and crossing our path. This chance sighting provided the by now almost routine mayhem in the cockpit. It was full throttle and I turned still on the deck, hoping to come up from below before we were spotted. We closed on the target as fast as we could, but just as we began to get in range the Condor lumbered into the low cloud. Frustrated, all I could do was follow and hope to pick him up emerging above or below the cloud.

Despite our best efforts we never regained the contact, though we did catch another fleeting glimpse of the aircraft through a break in the clouds. Eventually we gave the patrol up as a lost cause and returned to Sumburgh to await the second Blenheim that we had lost in the cloud. Once landed, we found out that they had in fact made a more eventful contact with the Condor. As the Condor finally emerged from the cloud, Rose and his crew were able to regain contact. Frantically fighting to get within range they finally put in an attack. Despite its size and lumbering pace, the Condor had fought back. Its rear gunner poured return fire into the attacking Blenheim, so much so that the British navigator was killed.

THE EARL OF ZETLAND

Despite having been at Sumburgh for some time, I had never actually seen the radar station on Unst. On the 22nd January 1941, I nearly missed the chance to change this. The problem was that they asked for a volunteer, and as you'd expect one of the first things you learn in the forces is that you never volunteer for anything unless you have the full facts. However, the weather at Sumburgh had taken a turn for the worse and flying was sporadic at best. So out of boredom more than interest I broke the golden rule and volunteered.

It turned out that they wanted someone to take a bundle of secret documents to the Unst radar post. As Unst was the most northern isle, this was to be no mean task. My first stop was in Lerwick were I spent the night. The next morning I turned up at the harbour to continue my journey. I felt all my enthusiasm for the trip drain away the moment I was greeted by the sight of the 'Earl of Zetland'. Once on board, the Captain explained to me that she was the oldest boat on the Lloyds register - and to my mind she certainly looked it!

It transpired that the 'Earl of Zetland' had been replaced in service just before hostilities started. With the outbreak of war, the government promptly requisitioned her replacement. In the meantime, the 'Earl' was rescued from the breakers yard at the last minute and pressed back into service. Her role was to ply the eastern seaboard of the Shetland Isles carrying mail and general provisions between the various fishing villages and islands.

Initially the journey proved faultless, especially to a hardened 'landlubber' like myself. The sea was reasonably calm while we remained in the lea of Whalsey Island. Once we broke out from its cover, things rapidly went downhill. A biting northeast wind hit the 'Earl' and she started to rock. Whilst I stayed on deck I was able to keep things under control. However,

During many of my earlier wartime postings, such as at Sumburgh, I often encountered standards of accommodation that could be classed as 'lacking'. Here is an excellent view of RAF tented accommodation, taken at St. Athans

I made the mistake of retiring inside and trying to eat. Going several shades of green, I was only marginally successful at preventing myself from being extremely ill. Eventually, despite the best efforts of Mother Nature, I reached Unst and delivered my cargo safely to the crew of the radar station. Only the return journey now awaited me!

ICE

A few days before my trip on the 'Earl of Zetland' I had an experience that was to have a lasting effect on me for the remainder of the war. Indeed, the results of this fright were not really cured until I did an instrument training course in 1949!

The Squadron had received supplies of a new secret material that was supposed to prevent ice forming on the leading edges of an aircraft's wing. Arriving in the form of a paste, its application was easy, simply being smeared along the wing's edge. Ignoring, once again, the basic service rule of never volunteering, I offered my plane as a test bed for the paste.

A 254 Squadron Mark IV Blenheim rests outside a hanger before undergoing a routine inspection.

The date of the test was the 12th January 1941, and with Tom Beale as passenger, I took off and headed out to sea.

The weather was pretty normal for the Sumburgh area. There was a thick cloud layer and its ragged base started at about 2,000ft. I took our Blenheim straight into this darkened mass. Almost immediately I realised how difficult the flying conditions were within the billowing clouds. The Blenheim was being thrown about in all directions. I was rapidly becoming disorientated, and equally began to realise that my instrument flying skills was not that good!

With each gyration I lost further track of the horizon, our height and our direction. I was also starting to over-correct - a mistake that was further compounded each time. The final straw came when both Tom and I were thrown from our seats and the engines hesitated. The plane emerged from the cloud base heading vertically down to the sea.

Tom grabbed the stick and tried to haul it as far back as possible. I had already managed to do this and we finally pulled out from the dive a mere 30 feet above sea level!

However, there was still time for further trouble. At the very point when the Blenheim's engines started to pull the plane out of the dive there had been a sharp crack followed by a muffled roar. Accompanied by a gust of freezing wind my side window ripped itself from the cockpit frame and disappeared behind us - thankfully missing the tailplane.

By now both Tom and I were extremely shaken, and it was with much trepidation that we headed straight back to Sumburgh. From that moment on I tried to avoid clouds like the plague. As for the paste, it had been forgotten in the chaos and the task of its evaluation was passed on to some other poor sole!

STING IN THE TAIL

During April 1941, someone at Group or Command came up with a new, and somewhat novel, anti-Condor idea. It consisted of an aircraft being dispatched to one of the Norwegian airfields from which the Condors operated, reaching it just before first light. Circling some

Trying my hand at air-to-ground photography using a rear facing camera. We are followed by another Blenheim which can just be seen in the distance.

distance from the airfield, the Blenheim would occasionally swing in over the German runway and drop a 20lb bomb. The theory was to disrupt the daily activities of the German airfield, thereby interrupting the departure of a Condor and reducing its daylight operating hours over the Atlantic.

On the 17th April I was assigned to one of these missions - only the third aircraft to be so honored! Taking off late on the evening of the 17th, it was 01.30 hours on the 18th when we landed at Wick to refuel. A brief chat with the ground crew and a welcome mug of tea was all we had time for before we were once again airborne.

It was a dark night, no moon and thick cloud. This meant that there was no visible horizon over the sea. Mindful of my 'paste' experience, I was soon sweating profusely and beginning to stiffen up. I realised, quite sensibly, that I was not going to be able to instrument fly for any greater length of time without getting into serious difficulties. For my own and my crew's sake the decision was made to return to Wick. Even the simple manoeuvre of turning for home was soon found to be not so simple. The 180-degree change in direction had to be made in a series of smaller turns. Each turn involved a few degrees change in course then straightening out, gathering our bearings and then another few degrees change. Were we glad to eventually find the runway lights at Wick! The condor patrols, in whatever form, continued unabated throughout April. On the 29th, a number of us were sent north from Unst to try to find a plane that had failed to return from one such patrol. The radar station, who also provided the news that they believed Butch had made contact with a Condor they had been tracking, had given us a rough location. It was at this point that his plane had disappeared from their screen.

Sadly we found no trace of his Blenheim, though at one stage I thought I had been in luck. I had spotted splashing, and banked my plane down towards sea level. I was right - there had been splashing - but sadly it turned out be a school of porpoises. Butch's loss seemed to confirm our growing theory that the Condors had been equipped with a large calibre machine-gun for their rear defence.

ATLANTIC CONVOYS

With the approach of spring 1941, we saw a gradual increase in the number of convoy patrols that the Squadron was assigned to. These were by no means boring - every convoy differed in size, composition and direction. You never knew what was going to happen next! For example, on the 13th March, one patrol saw us covering an Atlantic Convoy of 45 ships. This was in fact a reasonably large convoy, and coupled with the fact that the ships were spread out, meant that each patrol circuit took quite a long time.

By the spring of 1941 much of 254 Squadron's time was spent on convoy escort work. This photograph of an Allied convoy, entering the Irish Sea on the final leg of its crossing, shows how the merchant vessels were arranged in a convoy.

Equally, not all patrols were carried out in a calm and collected manner. On the 26th March, I had to hurry to get off to a convoy as the Unst radar post reported that it had picked up the presence of a Condor that was making directly for a convoy. No sooner had I arrived and started to gather my bearings when we were ordered to return immediately to Sumburgh as it was felt that the weather was about to close there. As we approached the airfield, we found that this was certainly not the case - indeed the weather had been worse over the convoy we had just left. Just as we began discussing the merits of the meteorological staff, the radio burst in and directed us to yet another Condor contact - they were obviously keeping themselves busy today! Banking round, we headed back out over the sea once again. This time we did find that the weather was worsening, and eventually gave up the hunt and returned to Sumburgh.

Early in April we again suffered at the hands of the weather, being unable to locate one particular convoy due to thick cloud. It was only after much discussion over the radio that we were able to get an exact position. Having found a convoy other, somewhat unexpected, dangers might await you. One particular Atlantic patrol, on the 21st April, provided proof of this.

Although the patrol had started in the usual manner - dense cloud cover - we did eventually stumble across the convoy. I approached carefully, and instructed my navigator to flash the identification letter of the day on his Aldis lamp. To support this, we also fired off two-colour cartridges from the Very pistol that gave the colours of the day. Having done this we went back around and tentatively tried to get a bit closer. No sooner had we done this than a couple of the ships in the convoy opened fire! Hotly pursed by anti-aircraft fire we banked away, making the mental note that we should provide the naval gunners with recognition charts that showed the difference between a 4-engined Condor, and our far smaller 2-engined Blenhiems!! As they were going to be unfriendly, my crew and I decided to leave the ships to it, and headed for home.

THE POSTER

On the 28th May 1941, we left Scotland and headed out over the Irish Sea to our new home. In an effort to get a rest from the Norwegian reconnaissance flights we had been posted to Aldergrove, near Belfast in Northern Ireland. Within hours of our arrival we were introduced to an official military photographer who, much to our amusement was attached to our flight. For the next few days it seemed that everything we did or everywhere we went we were accompanied by the clicking of a camera shutter! We were even instructed to do some formation flying

The Poster! This picture, taken by an official war photographer at RAF Aldergrove, soon appeared on billboards across Great Britain. Bill Sise is on the far right.

for him. To start with this was a novel experience, though very rapidly deteriorated into an annoying irritation. On one occasion my crew and Bill Sise's, were pictured near our aircraft. What seemed a relatively innocuous act at the time was soon to come back and haunt us!

Some weeks later a couple of RAF friends of mine had returned to London on some well earned leave. They had stopped to admire a new RAF recruitment poster that had suddenly sprung up on many of the nation's billboards. Taken aback by the surprise, they immediately realised that the stars of this poster were none other than my crew and I! Needless to say, and in the true nature of the Armed Services, it was to be some time before the rest of the Squadron finally put this matter to rest!

A few days after our arrival at Aldergrove, I was involved in an unpleasant incident. On the 16th July we were ordered out on another Convoy patrol. I commenced take-off and began accelerating down the runway. Our speed increased until we were doing almost 80 miles an hour. At this point the port tyre burst, and all hell broke loose. Slamming on the starboard brake I tried to hold the aircraft's course. Unable to maintain a straight line, the plane turned off the runway. The port wheel dug into the soft ground, and the port undercarriage leg was ripped off. In a flash, Foster and I climbed out of the cockpit roof and Tyson out of the rear hatch, all of us not a little unconcerned that we were sitting on a full fuel load. As I tumbled out of the plane I had felt a tug on the back of my helmet, and it wasn't until we had calmed down that I found out why. In our adrenaline enhanced panic to vacate the plane I had forgotten to disconnect my helmet's R/T plug. So there I was, standing by the runway, trailing a cable on the end of which was the actual plug and wiring mounting, freshly ripped from the Blenheim's cockpit!

FENCE POSTS

Our time at Aldergrove had partly been intended as a rest - or R&R as we

called it. Our accommodation was good, and the mess equally so. Rhona and I were in the wing of a large farmhouse in Crumlin. Entry was gained by hiking up some steps on which could always be found resting chickens, before climbing over the kitchen windowsill. Equally, large numbers of turkeys that could be found roosting in surrounding trees, inhabited the whole area. Another treat was the cooker - a valor paraffin stove that had the worrying habit of smoking badly! Sometimes we would be sitting in the sitting room, when you

An aerial photograph of the Coastal Command airfield at Aldergrove, Antrim, Northern Ireland. This is now the civil airport for Belfast, which is some 13 miles to the southeast.

would become aware of black specks in the air. We would rush into the kitchen and find it full of dense smoke.

Determined to make the most of this more relaxed posting, we took the opportunity to visit the surrounding countryside. Such trips though, still provided us with much excitement. One night we had driven into Belfast to a party. On the return, late at night, I was following a friend of mine who was driving his Singer Coupé. Making our way through the black out Charlie saw a red light waving at the side of the road. Thinking it was someone trying to hitch a lift, and conscious that his car was already full, he decided not to stop. Passing the person waving the light he got the fright of his life when shots were fired after him. He put his foot hard down and sped off down the road, weaving from side to side! It was the Police, manning a temporary checkpoint, who had tried to stop Charlie. We found it very strange to see British policemen with revolvers at their side.

Further four wheeled mishaps were to follow. Returning from a dining in night, I had turned into the long gravel drive that led to our billet at Glendaragh Farm. My Austin Nippy seemed to be going well, and I may well have been making the most of the deserted track. As I motored down the drive I came to a sharp bend. The car skidded on the gravel and I lost control. Bouncing onto the grass I was able to stop the car. The only problem was that I had managed to get it wedged between two solid looking fence posts. I trudged up the rest of the drive in the moonlight and, feeling somewhat guilty, crept in through the bedroom window. The next morning I expected to be confronted by an irate farmer, but instead he ended up apologizing for a tricky drive. He said that the same thing had happened to others before me. Thankfully the car had also escaped being damaged.

REPULSE AND NELSON

Despite the partying we did at Aldergrove, there was still work to be done. On the 31st August we were sent to escort another large Atlantic convoy. We were told that it contained a large number of naval vessels, which did nothing to settle our nerves. Our experiences told us that the higher the number of naval vessels, the greater the amount of itchy trigger fingers! However, as we closed in on the massed shipping, an impressive sight greeted us. In the middle of the convoy, ploughing along at full steam was the battleship HMS Repulse. She presented a truly inspiring sight. The sea was rough, so much so that waves were breaking right over the prow and rolling down the deck to crash up against the

Taken high over the Northern Ireland countryside, this photograph shows Blenheim Mark IVs of 'A' flight 254 Squadron. Bill Sise's aircraft is the one nearest mine.

first of the massive gun turrets. On the 21st November, we repeated the experience with another convoy, though this time it was the battleship HMS Nelson. Interestingly, on this occasion we had used a narrow air corridor that stretched westwards over neutral Eire. The Irish authorities allowed us to use this route to reach convoys that were west or southwest of Aldergrove. In doing so we were saved from flying north, avoiding the northern part of Eire. This permitted greater time in the air above the convoys.

Lough Neagh was close to the airfield and was frequently used to practice low flying. This was particularly the case after an aircraft had been through an inspection, to see whether it was upto scratch on speed. On one occasion, when the water was particularly flat, I nearly came unstuck. I was attempting to get as low as possible when water splashed up onto the windscreen. I yanked the stick back, and immediately had to throttle one engine right down as it was vibrating. I landed back at Aldergrove, and had to apologise to the ground crew for bending the propellers! I was amazed to find that on one of the propellers, only two of the three blades had been bent. It was this that had caused the vibration, not a damaged engine.

Also near the airfield, and alongside Lough Neagh, was a golf course that was frequently used by the station staff. On one particular day, I had the task of flight testing a Blenheim whilst Ken and some of the others had gone off for a few rounds of golf. Banking round the edge of the lake, I spotted them on a hole right beside the water. I couldn't resist it. Opening the throttle wide, I edged the nose of the plane down and dived in for a very fast, and equally low, pass. They were most indignant, accusing me of making them lose a ball. Ducking at the most inopportune moment, they had taken their eyes off the ball, which had promptly sailed off into the rough!

TRAGEDY

In September 1941, the rank of the Commanding Officers of twin engined squadrons was upgraded to Wing Commander. In line with this, Flight Commanders were to be elevated to Squadron Leaders. So it was that on

More low-level training, and two more air-to-ground pictures. This time the targets are a church and a village high street.

the 13th September, as acting leader of 'A' Flight, I was promoted to acting Squadron Leader. Soon after, I was to get a taste of the responsibility that such a rank bestowed.

Ever since we had arrived at Aldergrove we had come to realise that discipline was somewhat lax. This was particularly noticeable in relation to flying duties. The main culprits here were the crews in the Hudson Squadron also based at Aldergrove. They had fallen into the habit of beating up the airfield when they returned from a sortie. Some of our new pilots had taken to emulating these acts. On this particular day one of our Blenheims was returning from a convoy patrol and decided to have a go at beating up the airfield. The consequences were tragic. He dived down towards the control buildings at full throttle, obviously intent on getting as low as he dared. The plane sank at the end of the approach, his tail plane hitting a telegraph pole. Out of control the plane crashed into the ground, plummeting through the kitchens of the NAAFI. This act of recklessness had cost the lives of all the crew of the plane, as well as four girls who had been working in the NAAFI at the time. For us newly promoted Squadron Leaders it provided a stark reminder of our need to control those pilots in our respective flights.

Four weeks after the crash, our Squadron was posted back to Dyce. I was lucky as I could make the journey by air. My new wife Rhona, however, had the dubious pleasure of driving our car there! She started off in convoy with two others, but after the crossing via Larne and Stranraer, she lost them somewhere in Scotland. After reaching the lowlands near Falkirk she thought it was starting to get misty. In fact, the radiator had started boiling, followed closely by the engine seizing up. Fortuitously, a local contractor came to her aid. He took her home for tea before putting her on a train to Aberdeen. He also got his local garage to fix the car. A few days later we travelled by train to Falkirk to collect it, deciding to stay overnight in the town. Arriving at the hotel we became acutely embarrassed whilst standing at the reception desk. Waiting with a single, small overnight bag, it became immediately apparent that the old ladies sitting around were obviously of the opinion that this was a one-night stand!

CHAPTER FIVE - **THE WAR YEARS 1942**

WHAT GOES UP...

During the first few days of January 1942 we were kept busy on convoy escort duties. There were also a couple of air sea rescue searches - something that was becoming a greater part of our workload. The first of these flights was for the crew of a Beaufighter that had gone down, whilst the second was an attempt to locate some rafts from a wreck. In both cases, the searches proved unsuccessful.

With the conditions finally improving, and the runways cleared after a monumental effort by all available staff, I take off at the controls of the first aircraft to leave Dyce for nearly two weeks.

As January progressed the weather deteriorated. In fact, the conditions became so severe that all flying ceased between the 14th and 30th of the month. It started snowing, and then kept on snowing. Up to the 14th, flying had already become increasingly irregular. The snow continued to pile up on the runways, and the effort to keep the Blenheims airborne involved more and more people. Eventually, everyone except for a few essential people, such as the cooks, had been put to work shoveling the

Before the flight shown over page the whole airfield had become snowed in. Even my little Austin Nippy fell victim, and no amount of frantic shoveling seemed to help!

snow off the taxiways and runway! Even such monumental efforts finally proved fruitless against the worsening elements, and all flying was postponed. One evening, Bill Barns and I armed ourselves with a couple of shovels and decided to make an attempt to reach our homes in Aberdeen. We dug the Austin out of several drifts, but eventually had to abandon it having only just reached the road that connects the airfield to the main road. Refusing to give up we continued on foot through strong winds and driving snow, finally emerging on the main road near a bus stop. No sooner had we stopped to gather our strength, a bus pulled up in front of us. When we arrived at the flat our wives were most unimpressed with our stories of arctic hardship - the buildings in the town had broken up the wind and drifting snow. Thankfully we were to be exonerated, a few weeks later the local paper reported it had been the worst blizzard for over 50 years.

Whilst the airfield remained snow bound, Bill Sise's Blenheim was taken into the hangers for a stern change. Without an aircraft, he was sent on leave so that when it finally reemerged it fell to me to give it a test flight. Taking the station Padre as the only passenger I pulled out onto the freshly cleared runway. As we lifted into the bracing air, it dawned on us that we were the first aircraft to take off from Dyce for just over two weeks. In fact, it was such a momentous event that the station photographer turned out to record the moment for prosperity!

...MUST COME DOWN

Almost as soon as we had started down the runway, I began to get the feeling that something was not quite right. The Blenheim was taking a lot of nose down trim on this take off, despite the fact that I had wound on the usual amount. As the speed built up the aircraft still felt tail heavy forcing me to wind on even more. By this time we had got too far into the take off to abort, leaving us no alternative but to continue. As the plane lifted into the air I was pushing hard on the stick with both hands. I found that I even needed both of my feet on the column to help keep the aircraft's nose from coming up. Needless to say, this method of take-off did not appear in the pilot's notes!

The take off might have been photogenic - but not so the landing. Here the Blenheim rests unceremoniously in the snow-covered fields of a Scottish farm.

I shouted at the Padre who, no doubt, now realised that things were not going quite according to plan. He was able to squeeze himself down onto the cockpit floor - not to pray, but to help push on the control column.

Struggling to maintain control I suddenly noticed that in his haste to help, the Padre was pushing on the rudder bar. Shouting at him in somewhat unclerical terms, I told him to help push on the control column. Despite our combined efforts I knew I would not be able to prevent the aircraft from stalling for much longer. My only option now was a crash landing.

One of the few patches of cockpit that could still be seen amongst the snowdrift into which I had managed to pile the Blenheim. Note the cartoon nose art that Bill had had painted on his aircraft.

Seeing what appeared to be a large flat field I throttled back and told the Padre to hang on. Just as the aircraft was about to impact, the realization dawned that the field was in fact a small hillock. Even worse, the undercarriage was still down.

In the fight to stay airborne I had forgotten this part of a take-off, let alone find a spare hand to pull it up! As we hit the ground both of the undercarriage legs folded allowing the plane to slide along on its belly, snow spraying up in all directions. Coming to a rest still in one piece, the Padre and I both took a moment to consider an old aviation saying. That is, if you can walk away from a landing, then it was a good landing!

Above: Soldiers, or local Home Guard, stand watch as RAF mechanics ponder the question of recovering the aircraft from what could only be described as a somewhat inaccessible location.

Below: Having climbed on the fuselage I was able to photograph the inside of the snow covered and somewhat battered cockpit.

STRONG TEA

Extricating ourselves from the now less than happy looking Blenheim, the Padre and I checked ourselves for injuries. We had both survived with little more than a few scratches. The aircraft though, was in a far more sorry state. Both of the engines had been ripped from their mountings - indeed one could be found lying a little way behind us. The cockpit was completely smashed up; a fact that made us even more pleased with our meagre collection of scratches. Both of the wings also looked as if they would never take to the air again.

Beginning to feel the effects of the biting cold wind, we trudged our way over to a nearby farmhouse. The occupants, plainly aware of our unorthodox arrival, welcomed us inside. Establishing that the farmer had no telephone I told the Padre that he would have to go and summon help. I felt it was my duty to stay and guard the wreckage. Muttering under his breath, the Padre again stepped out into the cold wind and snow, following the farmer's directions to the nearest phone. I made myself comfortable in the warm cosy kitchen, establishing myself near the window so as to be able to keep at least one eye on the aircraft. Then the tea started to flow, leaving me to feel slightly guilty at sending the Padre off! The tea was some of the strongest that I had ever had. It seemed that the teapot sat permanently on the stove, with more water and tea simply added at regular intervals. After several cups of this very strong tea, the farmer reappeared in the kitchen. He wanted to know what I wanted to do about the petrol that was leaking from one of the fuel tanks. He must have thought that Christmas had come early for I told him that he could do what he liked with it. Needing no second bidding, the farmer and his son ran round gathering every single bucket, tin and container that they could muster before filling them up with the leaking fuel. Once they had finished, I warned them to mix the fuel with normal pool petrol, for the stuff we had been carrying in the plane was 100 octane. Using this neat in a normal tractor or car engine could well have had dire consequences.

After a few more hours, help arrived in the form of the Squadron C.O., some of my fellow pilots and a stretcher party. Highly amused at the sight of these 'rescuers', I told them that if I had seen them coming earlier, then I would have laid down beside the aircraft, pretended to have been injured and let them carry me back. As it was, having thanked the farmer for his hospitality, we all walked back through the snow to the road and our waiting transport.

Another view (above) of the battered airframe. In the background is the welcoming farmhouse where I consumed gallons of tea whilst the Padre staggered around the countryside trying to contact the airfield. Could this (below) have been the cause - reversed trim tabs (circled)?

SNOWBALLS

Once back on the airfield we were able to reassess what had gone wrong with the aircraft. It seemed strange that only a few days before we had all been in the mess discussing a similar incident. In this case the stern frame on a Blenheim had broken, jamming the elevator controls. I therefore began to assume that the stern frame on Bill's aircraft had not been mended correctly. This then caused it to break and in turn affect the elevators. It was not until the wreckage was removed from the crash site that the truth was found. It transpired that the elevator trim tabs had been wired up incorrectly so that they were in fact reversed. I had therefore been winding on 'tail down trim', when I thought I was doing 'nose down trim'. This would explain why I had such difficulty in trying to prevent the aircraft from stalling.

To celebrate the successful crash landing, a number of us decided to have a night out in Aberdeen. Everything went smoothly until the others decided to make their way back to Dyce by taxi. Every single taxi driver they asked refused, citing the snow as their reason. After an hour or so of unsuccessful taxi hailing, all conducted in the freezing cold, it was decided that everyone should come back to our flat. We staggered along, snow balling any taxi that we saw. One of the others also decided to collect a Belisha beacon as a souvenir!

DONALD DUCK

At the beginning of February 1942, Number 254 Squadron Coastal Command was posted to the airfield at Carew Cheriton in Pembrokeshire. As soon as we arrived we were given a new and somewhat different task to undertake. We were to escort a civilian Douglas D.C.3 passenger aircraft to a point west of the French port of Brest. The reason for these patrols had their origins in an event that occurred some time previously. One of these civilian flights, previously unescorted, had been intercepted by German aircraft during the flight and shot down over the Bay of Biscay. One of the passengers on this ill-fated flight that had been on route to Gibraltar was the film star Leslie Howard.

Donald Duck adorns the nose of this Blenheim, - the aircraft carried the code letter 'D' for Donald.

Each of these escort duties followed the same pattern. Firstly the two assigned aircraft would fly over to Chivenor on the North Devon coast where they would land and refuel. Here we would also meet up with the Dakota and its passengers. Whilst the latter were in a rest hut drinking coffee, we would look inside the passenger aircraft to find evidence that one of those aboard might be a glamorous young female. The pilots would then toss a coin to see who would have the pleasure of formating on that side of the D.C.3! Once all three aircraft were airborne, the Blenheims would take up station on either side of the passenger plane. The cabin curtains were kept drawn, for security reasons, until all the aircraft were well out of sight of land. It was then that they were drawn back. It was amusing to see the reactions of the various passengers when they saw these Blenheims tucked in so close.

On the 10th March 1942 my aircraft, 'D' for Donald, was finally fitted with a bulletproof windscreen. I well remember that most of us greeted their arrival with the reaction 'better late than never'. After all, the war had only been going for three years! We were lucky that amongst the squadron's ground crew was a very good artist. As a result many of our Blenheims were decorated with various Disney characters. Being 'D' for Donald, my aircraft was adorned with a Donald Duck figure, his fists raised defiantly in the air.

CRASH LANDING TWO

A No. 254 Squadron Blenheim (K-QY) having over-run the runway at Carew Cheriton.

CRASH LANDING THREE

Further carnage. In this case though the force of impact appears to be greater, with the aircraft suffering more extensive damage. Judging by the state of the remains it is almost certain that the aircraft would have been written off and the airframe cut up and sent for salvage.

The top picture clearly shows how the aircraft has broken its back with the nose pointing downhill. The leading edges of the wings are torn to shreds, possibly after contact with small trees or shrubs. Surprisingly the engines seemed to have remained fixed to their mountings, though the propellers are all bent and twisted. This is characteristic of a crash in which the propellers are still turning at the moment of impact. This happened near Dyce.

Preparing to be taken out to the aircraft for a mission. This crewman is holding his parachute in his right hand.

During our time at Carew Cheriton we carried out some naval co-operation flights, assisting a number of anti-aircraft ships that were moored in Milford Haven. The idea was to make feint attacks on the ships from a variety of different directions and speeds. Flying in at low level both from land and from out at sea was to provide everyone involved with much enjoyment. It was also pleasing to know that for once we could approach the Royal Navy without the possibility of being fired upon! To say thank you, the Navy threw a party for us aboard one of the ships. There were only two drinks on offer - 'Gremlins Blood' and 'Thunder Clap'. Both concoctions were extremely potent, and to this day I have never found out the substances from which they were produced! Once the party came to an end, the senior service provided us with one last test. In order to get back to shore we needed to descend down to our launch via a rather long rope ladder. To add further spice to the proceedings it was a dark night, the ship was rolling at anchor and the quantities of unknown alcoholic drinks consumed did nothing to provide a clear and sharp mind. Thankfully no one was beaten, and no matter how long it took, all us 'aviation' types did make dry land without getting wet.

On the 15th April I was sent to provide cover to a cable laying ship that was accompanied by a naval escort. Formating with the ships off the south coast of Eire I was leading the second Blenheim. As we finished one particular pass I was absolutely amazed to see what appeared to be a German Condor approaching the convoy from the west. I mentally crossed myself, opened the throttles and pulled +9. In the headphones I could hear the second pilot, Johnny Lowe, shouting that he was right behind me. We climbed as fast as we could, forcing our engines to get us into a position where we could attack the German out of the sun. Not wishing to miss my opportunity I banked my aircraft round and started to sweep into a quarter attack on the enemy. Thankfully my shooting was of its usual poor standard, for as I opened fire I realized that the 'Condor' had twin rudders. I had in fact just attacked a friendly aircraft!

Once I had returned to Carew with my tail firmly between my legs, I was able to find out more. The plane I had thought was a German Condor was in fact a De Havilland Albatross. This very rare British aircraft was on its routine daily flight from Shannon in Eire to the British mainland. Intelligence had told us nothing about this, though I should have guessed by the simple fact that the naval gunners had stayed steadfastly silent during the 'enemy's' approach!

UNFRIENDLY WELCOME

One of the last pictures I was to take of Blenheims flying in formation.

Late in April 1942, it was the turn of one of the other pilots, Bill Sise, to provide the Squadron with its latest source of amusement. The whole episode had started off as nothing more than a routine convoy escort flight. Operations had told Bill that the ships were to be found southwest of Eire, well out into the Atlantic. Arriving at the expected location of the convoy Bill and his crew were greeted by nothing except the sight of a completely empty sea. Flying in circles, Bill tried to locate the ships, and still having no luck they resorted to a creeping line ahead search. Even these measures proved fruitless, and somewhat fed up, Bill asked for a course for home. It was at this point that the problems started.

Sadly Bill had a navigator who could not have been classed as one of the best. Throughout the time that the aircraft had been searching over the Atlantic he had made a near fatal error. He omitted to check on the wind's speed, direction and strength by taking drifts. Even when he supplied Bill with the course for home he did not realise his mistake. Eventually land was sighted and the crew began to relax in anticipation of a hearty meal in the mess. By the navigator's estimation they were crossing the English coast somewhere in Cornwall, and they banked round to fly west along the shore. Bill then spotted a floatplane sitting on the beach, and its unfamiliar shape began to concern him. Just as the realization began to dawn, heavy anti-aircraft fire opened up on them. The floatplane was a German He-115, and the shoreline had nothing to do with England. Indeed, Bill's plane had crossed the French coast just south of Brest. As the anti-aircraft fire slammed into his aircraft, Bill raced out to sea vehemently cursing his navigator. Despite being hit and damaged Bill returned the crew to Carew shaken, but thankfully unharmed.

A few days later, on the 4th of May, another one of the Squadron's aircraft got into difficulty. This time the results were more tragic. The other flight commander had gone on a Dakota escort and had been forced to take a replacement aircraft as his normal one went U/S. For some reason both of their engines must have cut out for the plane ditched near Lundy Island. It must have been extremely sudden, for there had not been the chance to send out a SOS. The alarm was not raised until the Blenheim became overdue at Chivenor. The rest of the Squadron was scrambled to search for the aircraft, but our efforts were hampered by thick sea mist.

Four hours later the pilot and navigator were picked up by an air sea rescue launch. The third crewman Bill Barnes, a good friend of mine, was never found. Sadly, both of the survivors later died from the effects of exposure.

Things then went quiet for a while, and on the 22nd June we started to convert to Beaufighters. On the 10th July, I was posted to No. 5 O.C.U. at Turnberry. Leaving No. 254 Squadron was a sad day. I had enjoyed flying the Blenheim, and my logbook showed that I had flown 630 hours in the type. 20 of these were at night, and 429 were so called operational hours.

No. 5 O.C.U (Operational Conversion Unit) at Turnberry was a Hampden and Beaufort conversion unit. The Hampdens were ex-Bomber Command and seemed to be pretty tired. They were to be used in Coastal Command as torpedo bombers. I was posted into Turnberry as Chief Ground Instructor. To say that this did not please me would be a huge understatement. I knew the sum total of nothing when it came to torpedo bombing, and having had all possible experience of long range fighter work I thought that it would have made more sense to have been posted to Catfoss to instruct on Beaufighters. Nevertheless, I had to put up with the infinite wisdom off those in charge and settled down to make the most of my time at Turnberry.

Wartime training units used a variety of aircraft types. Shown here is an Airspeed AS.10 Oxford. This was a two-seat general-purpose trainer, which remained in service until 1954. By then some 8,586 had been built.

I found that Turnberry was not a very happy station. There seemed to be a lot of unnecessary restrictions placed on the pupils. I felt that life should have been made easier for them as the job they were training for was dicey to say the least. Worse, the aircraft that they flew were old, tired and accident-prone hand-me-downs gathered from other parts of the RAF. One example of the trivial regulations that awaited the new pupil was the fact that he was not permitted to take his service bicycle off the station. My efforts to overturn this rule fell on deaf ears. The new Station Commander had not been long in place and had other more important issues to contend with. The previous one, far more dictatorial, had earned himself the nickname of 'The Praying Mantis'. It had become his habit to have prayers said over the airfield tannoy system after every fatal accident, which at the time was fairly frequent.

Despite all this I was able to get some flying done soon after my arrival. There were two trips in a Hampden, followed by an outing in an old battered Avro Anson. During this flight I took some pupils on a bombing practice, trying to hit a towed target at low level. Bill Sise took me in a Beaufighter to do a practice torpedo attack in the Clyde approaches. This, however, only wetted my appetite to escape from Turnberry and return to long range fighters. My wish was soon to be realized, for on the 28th August 1942 I was indeed posted to Catfoss and its Beaufighters.

CATFOSS

Soon after my arrival at No.2 O.C.U Catfoss, I found that the Beaufighter was a far more powerful aircraft than the Blenheim. It also packed a greater punch. This combination also meant that the Beaufighter was more of a handful for us pilots. Even getting into the plane was a feat in itself. A trap door opened in the bottom of the fuselage. In full kit, you had to clamber up a thin ladder attached to the trap door, through an even slimmer hatch, and then climb over the back of the seats into the cockpit. The navigator/wireless operator who sat further back down the fuselage had a similar procedure with his own hatch.

Once at the controls, most other problems were related to the aircraft's engines. The Beaufighter was equipped with two powerful Bristol Hercules units. Attach these to a fuselage slimmer than that of the Blenheim and you are left with an interesting combination. The huge engines required large propellers to absorb the power. Consequently the

The Bristol Beaufighter, which I first came across on my arrival at No.2 Operational Conversion Unit at Catfoss on the 28th August 1942.

undercarriage legs had to be long. This was to ensure that the props did not touch the ground when the aircraft was in the flying position, i.e. parallel to the ground. Therefore, the aircraft would stand with the fuselage at quite a large angle to the ground. On take off or landing, this meant that the plane had to move through this large angle to get from the tail down to the flying position. The two large propellers acted as gyroscopes and when they were moved through this angle a gyroscopic precession took place. The aircraft would swing to the left. You countered this by leading with the port throttle and use of the starboard rudder. On landing a similar but smaller effect was felt and was cured by just the use of the rudder.

Such problems gradually labelled the Beaufighter with a bad reputation among some of our pupils. The situation became so bad that one pupil finally refused to climb up the ladder into the cockpit, instead just clinging to it for all his worth. It took much persuasion before he finally let go. The medical people sadly classified him as "L.M.F", (Lack of Moral Fibre), and he was never to fly again.

A few days later we took delivery of a new Beaufighter. Following what can only be described as a demonstration of the perfect way in which to land a Beaufighter, the aircraft taxied into our dispersals. Eager to examine our new arrival we made our way over to the aircraft just in time for the ladder to drop down. Much to our surprise a tiny figure dressed in navy blue emerged. It was a female pilot from the A.T.A. To say that our jaws dropped would be an understatement! Surprisingly enough from this time on there were no more grumblings from our pupils!

WORKS & BRICKS

For a time now I had been living in the Mess. Indeed, as a result of this 'tenancy', I had been made the P.M.C. (President of the Mess Committee). We ran a suggestion book in which the others put ideas and requests for the Mess, and it was my task to try and implement those that seemed half-sensible. One afternoon I checked the book to find that the station medical officer had made an entry. Fed up at being gassed by all the smokers in the Mess, 'Doc' wanted to see better ventilation in the bar. Dutifully I made my way across to the administration block to take the matter up with 'works & bricks'. With little more than a blank expression they informed me that such jobs were not that high on their list of 'must-dos'!

A few nights later I was woken from a deep sleep by the most appalling racket. It sounded like a particularly heavy anti-aircraft barrage over Hull, which was nearby. Cursing the Luftwaffe I decided that as I was now awake I might as well go and see what was happening. I made my way along the corridor to the window at the top of the stairs where I could usually get a good view of any raid. Straining my eyes I was greeted by nothing more than the pitch black of night. There were no searchlights flickering, no flashes of bursting flak or even the dull glow of burning fires - just the awful racket. Now I realised the noise was coming from the direction of the bar!

Storming off to investigate, I went downstairs to the bar. At the bottom of the stairs I found the cause of the row. A saw blade was protruding through the panel wall that divided the bar from the stairway. I watched as the saw hacked back and forth. As I stood there the last part of a square was cut, and a section of the wall fell out. I popped my head through the gap, only to see the 'Doc' standing there, saw in hand, with a triumphant grin on his face!

More formation flying - though this time with a different aircraft. The Beaufighter had initially started out as a private venture design, sourcing some 75% of its parts from the earlier Bristol Beaufort. The only entirely new components were the engine mountings and the main fuselage section.

UCKERS

Our chief diversion in the flight office during poor weather and other slack moments was the game of Uckers. This was basically a more complicated version of Ludo. It was a team game that you played with your opposite number against another two. If my memory serves me right this was a game that had been poached from the Navy. I remember

Playing Uckers. This is basically a more complicated version of Ludo. It was a team game that you played with your opposite number against another two.

one game in particular. Bill Moore was vigorously shaking the dice and shouting for a number 6 when the door to the flight office flew open and in stormed the Group Captain. To say that Bill's jaw hit the deck would be an under statement! However, life at Catfoss was not all play and no work.

On the 31st July 1942 we carried out an air sea rescue mission. Two of us went as an escort for a Coastal Command Hudson that was equipped with an airborne lifeboat. Our task on this occasion was to try and find the crew of a bomber that had been forced to ditch in the North Sea. All the detail that we had been given was that their last known position was some way off the Dutch Coast.

Before we set off, one of us made a very poignant remark, both of the Beaufighters on the mission belonged to the Flying Training flight at Catfoss. As a result the guns were never fired, indeed there was a separate air firing training flight. There we were, heading south towards German occupied Europe as an escort for an even bigger aircraft, unsure whether or not our guns would fire! I took up position on the starboard side of the Hudson as we plugged on over the North Sea.

As we approached the search area, I casually glanced out of the window to ponder the bleakness of the water below thanking God that it wasn't me in the dinghy, when I suddenly saw them. We passed over with the dinghy passing between the Hudson and us, which was one hundred yards away on my left. Desperate not to lose sight of the stranded airmen, I turned and circled the dinghy. Simultaneously I fired off a couple of Very lights. As we began to circle above the dinghy we could do nothing but watch as the Hudson plodded on, seemingly unaware of the drama behind him. We cursed the wretched air gunner on the Hudson for he must have been out of his turret. All we could do was to keep circling whilst my navigator sent out our position on the W/T. I hoped this would be soon, and we all began to get a little tetchy. There we were, flying in ever decreasing circles close to occupied Europe, and the incumbent Luftwaffe, gaily transmitting our position. This coupled with the fact that we had no idea whether or not our guns would work meant that I found it somewhat difficult to relax.

Not before time, the Hudson and the other Beaufighter returned. It was the first time that I had seen an air sea rescue of this nature take place. It was fascinating to watch the Hudson go through its paces. Banking into its final approach the aircraft began to lose height and speed. Just as it passed over the dinghy it let the lifeboat go, and we watched as it sailed down beneath its own parachute. Full marks to the Hudson crew, for their aim was spot on. Bringing their dinghy alongside, the stranded bomber crew climbed in with little effort. As we continued to circle we watched as the airmen ditched the parachute and erected the lifeboat's mast. With this, it was time to leave, joining the Hudson for the return journey. To this day, I have never heard whether they got back to the UK safely.

CHAPTER SIX - **THE WAR YEARS 1943**

NIGHT FIGHTER

On the 19th February 1943 I was asked by an officer from Flight Engineering if I would go to Snaith and bring back a Night Fighter Beau' that needed to go to Catfoss for repair. It was thought to have under carriage faults, and therefore I had to fly the whole way with the under cart down. The journey up to Snaith was completely uneventful - the same could not be said of the return!

One of my colleagues, Bill Moore. Preparing for a flight Bill is wearing his RAF issue Irvine jacket.

Once airborne I decided that caution would be the order of the day. I treated the nightfighter gently, throttling back and opening the cooling grills to keep the engine temperatures down. Despite this, the temperature gauges gradually climbed up, so that the engines were reaching the level at which they ran the risk of cutting out. I was now concerned! We had some distance to go, so in an effort to try and cool the engines I raised the under carriage to increase the cooling airflow through the engines.

This seemed to work, for soon after we were able to join the circuit to land at Catfoss.

In preparation, I lowered the under carriage. Bad news, for the cockpit indicators showed me that the wheels had failed to lock! At this point I began to wonder if my service in the RAF would ever be straight forward and simple! I tried the emergency system, and this too failed. I came round on the approach once again, this time as low and as slow as I dared. This allowed the duty pilot on the ground a chance to make a visual examination. He backed up the cockpit instruments, telling us that the under carriage had indeed failed to lock completely down. After further fiddling with the undercarriage switches and much praying it would work we had to concede defeat. There was nothing for it but to make an emergency landing.

Choosing a stretch of grass beside the runway I surprised even myself by executing a perfect belly landing. We were even able to have a chuckle to ourselves - if the plane had needed repairing before, then it certainly did now. Despite our protestations, we were taken by ambulance to the sick quarters. Here the 'Doc' produced some tea and later something to help us sleep. Finally, back at our quarters we hit the sack and awoke the next morning to find that the 'Doc' had insisted on making regular visits throughout the night. It later transpired that he realised that he'd given us a much stronger dose of sleeping pills than he should have done!

THUNDER FLASHES

Later in the year I received a new posting. On November 15th I returned to active operations, joining No. 248 Squadron based at Predannack on the Lizard Peninsula. It was a very happy squadron, and there were a lot of good chaps on it. By nature of its location, most of the squadron's work involved patrols across the Bay of Biscay looking for German reconnaissance aircraft on their way out into the Atlantic. Despite the fact that the war had been going for nearly four years, I was once again back into hutted accommodation. Predannack was a busy airfield. With a Polish Wellington squadron, a Typhoon squadron, and a special flight of Mosquitos also based there.

I found a bungalow to rent right on the edge of the cliff path. One of the navigators, Bill Belcher, and his wife shared it with us. Bill was an incredibly interesting chap, and he and I would often go beach combing for wood. His father was a judge, and Bill had fought for the Communists in Spain against Franco. I remember one day a letter arriving from the Air Ministry security people requesting that the CO write a report about Bill because of his involvement in the Spanish Civil War. We were most indignant, and replied that, in case they hadn't noticed, we were all fighting Fascism now, the only difference being that Bill had been doing so for a lot longer!

The CO of No.248 Squadron was 'Monty' Burton. Apart from spending his whole time trying to get more exciting operations for the squadron, he was also a complete menace to his flight crews. He had developed the maddening habit of letting off thunder flashes in people's rooms. Thunder flashes are basically very large "bangers" used by the armed services. It wasn't long after my arrival that I suffered at Monty's hands. One evening, when I was relaxing in my room, he and a Flight Commander called 'Digger' Power came in, apparently for a chat. I should have guessed that something was up by the grins on their faces. Hardly saying a word, they bolted from my room, slamming the door in their wake. Wondering at this schoolboy behaviour, reality suddenly dawned when I saw a thunder flash resting on the floor with its fuse burning merrily. I only just had time to pull the bed clothes around me before the damn thing went off!

THE SUBMARINE

During November I was sent on a five-day detachment to Group Headquarters in Plymouth. Some bright spark at Group had come up with the idea that all Squadron and Flight Commanders should do this detachment so that they could get to know the staff at Group. Our party included the Squadron Leaders of three different anti submarine squadrons. This meant that, as well as a tour of the Operations Room, we also visited an actual submarine.

The submarine in question was in Plymouth, having come in for repairs. It's CO, a much-decorated Lieutenant, informed us that they had just returned from the Mediterranean. Here they had been employed in landing army saboteurs on the Italian coast. Its officers entertained us in

No.248 Squadron personnel photographed in front of a Beaufighter. This Coastal Command unit was originally established in August 1918.

the wardroom. Now we realised just how lucky we were - I thought we had a very jammy life in comparison. The wardroom was just like a third class railway compartment. The four or five officers on the submarine had to share this cramped area for weeks on end. As far as I was concerned they were welcome to it!

A number of drinks later, the Lieutenant informed us that the sub was about to go on a test dive. Needless to say all us aviation types were invited along for the ride. The drawback was that only three out of the four of us would be able to stay on board. Sensing my opportunity, and acting with speed that surprised even my colleagues, I very generously said that I would remain on shore. With a huge sigh of relief, I made my way across the gangplank to dry land. I had absolutely no desire to dive in a submarine!

BLOCKADE RUNNER

By December, we had received the news that we were going to be re-equipped with Mosquitos, and indeed I had my first flight in one on the

Having been re-equipped with Mosquitos it was time for another Squadron photograph. Clearly visible here are the twin 1,620hp Rolls-Royce 25 inline piston engines.

9th. The Mosquito was even better than the Beaufighter - we had come a long way since the early Tiger Moths that I had begun my service in. The Mosquito was faster and lighter on the controls. The Mosquito had four 20mm cannon, four .303 machine guns mounted in the nose and could carry two 500lb bombs in its bomb bay. It could also out turn a Beaufighter.

It was this last point that provided much mirth. One of the die-hard Beaufighter pilots refused to accept that the newcomer could out turn his beloved aircraft. I challenged him to a mock dogfight in an effort to prove my point. After we had landed, with victory having fallen to my Mosquito, his navigator staggered over. Still visibly shaking he reported that at one point the Beaufighter had been shuddering so badly he was sure that it would stall. Being shocked by the effects of trying to keep pace with the Mosquito, he had clipped himself into his parachute harness whilst clinging on for dear life!

On the 14th we were to become part of the hunt for a ship that been designated a class 1 target by the Admiralty. This was the 'Pietro Orsilo'. Under her Italian master, this ship had been successful in taking desperately needed supplies from Germany to Japan, and returning with full loads of rubber for the German war industries. The ship had been sighted moving westwards along the coast of Brittany, and so the chase was on. What we all thought would be a relatively simple operation turned out to be anything but! We had been detailed to escort four torpedo carrying Beaufighters of No. 254 Squadron who had been sent on detachment to Predannack for the sole purpose of sinking the blockade runner. In view of the density of German fighter bases in the area, our orders only permitted an attack if there was cloud cover. Needless to say, as we approached the target area, the cloud completely evaporated, forcing us to abort and return home.

Three days later, the conditions seemed suitable for another attempt. Everything was fine until about an hour into the flight. At this point one of my engines started to pop and bang. No manner of cursing or cajoling seemed to help, forcing me to turn for home. Failure number two!

The following day, the powers-that-be decided enough was enough. The blockade-runner had been tracked to a position west of the port of Concarneau. A smaller transport, a gaggle of M-class minesweepers, and a few flak ships accompanied her. An attack would be made today, whether there was or was not any cloud cover. As an extra measure, a larger force was assembled. This time six Torpedo Beaufighters, six of us and eight Typhoons, as top cover, started the journey south. We found the German convoy exactly where we expected. With the Typhoons staying above as the fighter cover, our Beaufighters dived in and attacked the minesweepers and flak ships, spraying them with cannon fire. Close behind the six torpedo carrying Beaufighters swept in low and level unleashing their torpedoes. Between them they scored two hits, and at long last the blockade running days of the 'Pietro Orsilo' were over.

A POLISH CHRISTMAS

Christmas was soon upon us, but far from being able to relax and enjoy ourselves, it seemed as if we would never step out of our Beaufighters! In fact, on Christmas Eve itself we saw some of the most frantic activity.

The de Havilland D.H.98 Mosquito has been called an aeroplane to be proud of, and like the Beaufighter was the result of a private venture. First flying in November 1940, by the end of production some 7,781 examples had been built.

The Admiralty had been receiving reports that another blockade-runner was on the loose in the Bay of Biscay. The only difference this time was that the German Navy had supplied some destroyers as an escort. Reinforcements of Beaufighters from Nos. 143 and 235 Squadrons along with another unit of Mosquitos and some fifteen Torbeaus arrived.

After a lot of changes of mind and numerous delays at Group we were eventually sent out to our aircraft at the dispersals. We sat in the cockpits awaiting the word to go, our aircraft fully loaded and ready for action. With the continued waiting, the nervous tension began to build. In fact it became so bad that my mouth became dry and I couldn't even spit sixpence! There was only one thing for it - I had to open the little tin of orange juice that I was supplied as a part of out in-flight rations.

Eventually we got going. There were nine aircraft from No. 248 Squadron (led by Monty), ten from both numbers 143 and 235, the twelve Mosquitos and fifteen Torbeaus (torpedo-carrying Beaufighters). Having managed to get all these aircraft into some semblance of order, we set off with one of the other Squadron Commanders leading. According to my navigator, Jimmy Bland, we all turned back some five minutes too soon. Indeed on landing we discovered that most of the other navigators concurred with Jimmy. Consequently, despite all the effort, nothing was seen.

On our return, the circuit at Predannock was distinctly crowded, with everyone waiting their turn to land. I kept right behind the CO, and eventually followed him in. One of the Beaufighters behind me was unlucky and had to go round again. As he did this Monty came up on the R/T and said "hard luck Tubby"! I quickly answered "keep going, I'm right behind you".

Eventually everyone got down onto the tarmac and in an effort to cheer us all up, the Poles invited us all to their mess for a Christmas party. It was a truly splendid evening, with the Poles even laying on a traditional Polish Christmas play. Only one person failed to enjoy herself - the head WAAF. Only too aware that her charges were quite susceptible to the Polish charm, she spent the entire evening keeping a weary eye on the ladies!!

LONE PATROL

The frantic pace did not ease much over the days following Christmas. On the 28th December, for example, I was ordered to take a patrol of 10 aircraft and provide an escort for some cruisers. Things followed the rather dismal pattern that had become almost the norm at this point. In their infinite wisdom, the Royal Navy did not provide us with the course of the ships, and despite our best efforts in searching the area indicated by Group, we were forced to give up and return to base empty handed.

Four days later, I carried out my last ever operational flight in a Beaufighter. Our route took us, alone, out across the Bay of Biscay as far as the Spanish coast and back. It was an uneventful flight until, on the return, we neared the French shore at Brest. There in front of us, lumbering along at its own pace in the middle of nowhere, was a Sunderland flying boat. Immediately it began flashing away at us with its Aldis signalling lamp. Intrigued, I tried to bring the Beaufighter alongside the Sunderland - no mean feat, I can tell you. Throttled right back, and with quite a bit of down flap, I was able to enter into some semblance of a formation with our bigger brother. Once alongside, the sheer size of this immense beast became all too apparent. Whilst I studied the flying boat, the navigator took down the message which was still being flashed out. It was 'Happy New Year'! Following a suitable reply, we peeled away, opened the throttles and continued on our journey home.

A few days later, I was at last able to enjoy a short break, as the squadrons had been stood down, and I decided to re-paint one of our Uckers boards. Sitting in the kitchen of our bungalow, the peace was shattered by the roar of a low flying aircraft. Almost simultaneously, the sound of cannon fire echoed through the building. Thinking that we were being attacked by German Focke-Wolf 190 fighters, I almost tripped over myself in the race to get outside. Bolting out through the back door, I just caught the tail end of the attacker as it banked away.

A superb view of the underneath of a Mosquito. In this view can be seen the four 20mm cannon that accompanied the nose mounted machine guns.

It was a Typhoon! It later transpired that this pilot had been tasked to test an aircraft. Bored, he had decided to wake the rest of us up. He had dived down the adjacent valley firing his guns out to sea, before banking round and flying adjacent to the cliff edge - guns still firing. The next morning the mess hall was full of extremely irritated and bruised airmen. Most had been dozing in bed only to be woken sharply by the cannon fire. Flinging themselves under their beds, almost all had picked up bruises along the way. Needless to say the pilot remained an unpopular chap for some time!

TSETSE PATROL

Before I left Predannack, I came into contact with a special flight of

Mosquitos. These were the aircraft of the Tsetse patrols. The Tsetse was a Mosquito that had been fitted with a huge 6lb anti-tank gun. It could fire eleven armour-piercing shells, capable of penetrating the hull of a submarine. The idea was that following the report of a U-boat leaving its base, such as Lorient, the Tsetse patrol would depart for an area search. The hope was to surprise the submarine still on the surface whilst still in the shallow inshore waters. The Tsetse aircraft would cause enough damage to prevent the U-boat from diving, allowing it to be finished off by an aircraft carrying bombs. Early in March 1944 we began to carry out routine patrols with the Tsetse flight. Normally two of our Mosquitos would accompany the Tsetse's, acting as their fighter and anti-flak escort.

An incredible picture that shows the Tsetse patrols at work. This is the U-821 on the day that it was caught on the surface and sunk - 10th June 1944. A type VIIC, launched on the 26th June 1943, she was lost along with all the crew except for one.

It was on one of these early joint patrols that I saw first hand the sheer power of the Tsetse guns. Flying in station on the port side of a Tsetse Mosquito, my aircraft suddenly shuddered. Simultaneously there was a loud bang. Jumping out of my skin, I thought that somehow an enemy fighter had managed to get behind me and launch an attack. I broke hard to port and opened the throttles. Then we noticed that the rest of the patrol was carrying on seemingly unconcerned. Finding the rest of the skies empty, I manoeuvred my Mosquito back into formation. Just as I came alongside the Tsetse, a puff of smoke emerged from its nose and once again I felt and heard a bang. I could very easily have hidden on the cockpit floor! There had been no enemy fighter, just the Tsetse testing his guns!

Soon after this, one of these Tsetse patrols had some action! A submarine was caught on the surface and was hit by the Tsetse. Winged and unable to dive, the U-boat could do little but wait as a nearby Coastal Command Liberator was called up. With the Tsetse patrol as a circling guard, the bomber took its time in setting up its approach. Its bombs were the last straw for the submarine, which started taking water. Its crew bailed out, taking to their dinghies. However, things did not end here. With our two Mosquitos and the Tsetse still watching, a German launch headed out from shore in a courageous attempt to rescue the submariners. There was no attempt to stop the rescue of the U-Boat crew, but one of the other Mosquitos strayed too close to the launch. A hail of anti-aircraft fire streamed up. Machine-gun bullets ripped into the aircraft's wing tip fuel tank. This exploded, tearing the Mosquito's wing off. Out of control, the plane spiraled down into the sea. Retaliating, the Tsetse shot at the launch, which rapidly sank.

CAUTIOUS QUEENIE

It was the very nature of our long-range operations that had led to the introduction of the wing tip fuel tanks that had cost one of our Squadron so dearly. The fuel they held was the first to be used, so that when you went into attack the theory was that they would be jettisoned. Whether empty or part full they were an obvious explosive risk. It was quite a sight on our later anti-shipping patrols to watch as they were released by an aircraft travelling low and fast.

During one of our combined Tsetse patrols, an incident occurred for which my navigator of the time, Jimmy Orchard, would never forgive me. It seemed as if the patrol was never ending, and possibly because of one too many pre-flight cups of tea, I developed a terrible need to spend a penny. There was nothing I did that would take my mind off it. I just had to go!

The author is shown here on the right, standing next to F/O Jimmy Orchard.

The Mosquito had a flexible metal tube, with a metal cup at the end that emerged from under the pilot's seat for just such an emergency. It was generally acknowledged though, that you had to be exceptionally desperate to avail yourself of this added extra. It was really easy to use, but you did need both hands free. Flying low and fast, I needed to keep one hand on the stick, so I nudged Jimmy and asked him to hold the cup in position. Unfortunately for him, there was a kink in the pipe, and by the time we both realised our mistake, everything was over-flowing. I was unable to stop! At least it was someone else's turn to do the cursing!

About this time we decided to apply nose art to some of our Mosquitos. Our plane carried the code letter 'Q'. So she became christened with the nickname 'Cautious Queenie', and keeping in line with the rest of the Squadron, one of the ground crew applied a suitable illustration. So our aircraft became adorned with a rear view of a buxom queen who was lifting her skirt to reveal a padlock on her underwear!

ENGINE FAILURE

March passed quickly, full of Tsetse patrols out over the Bay of Biscay. We had also moved to Portreath. It appeared to us that the Germans had become wise to our intentions, for despite spending a lot of time in the air, we achieved nothing but blank score sheets. On the 5th April 1944, 'Cautious Queenie' was called in for a modification to be carried out, and she was flown to Hatfield. On the 12th, my leave was interrupted by a message instructing me to go to Hatfield and collect 'Queenie'. The fact that I had no maps, and was not given one at Hatfield, did not overly concern me. The route back was straightforward. Taking off from Hatfield one aimed straight for the Bristol Channel. When you hit the

Another view of the sharp end of a Mosquito, behind 'Dobby' Dobson and his navigator

water, you simply turned left and followed the coast until the airfield at Portreath appeared!

On the 27th April, I was detailed to take part in a patrol along the south coast of the Brest peninsula. It was a mixed force consisting of six Beaufighters, six of our Mosquitos and two Tsetses. After a couple of hours into the flight, one of the Mosquitos developed an engine failure. I decided that, as this was a new pilot, I would escort him home, allowing the rest of the patrol to carry on. Once we were alone, we had another pressing problem. We were flying at a height that was too low if his other engine decided to give up the ghost and he would have to ditch. We needed to gain height. Not a huge problem except that this would bring us into view of the German coastal radar. However, there was nothing we could do, and I told the other pilot to gradually increase his altitude, but in so doing to try and not overstrain his sole remaining engine.

We hadn't gone far when Jimmy screamed into the RT. His keen eye had spotted six single engined aircraft closing fast astern. There we were, one and half against six, stuck out over the Bay of Biscay! Fearing the worst, we decided that attack would be the best form defence. If nothing else, it might at least allow the other Mosquito to slip away. Preparing ourselves, we executed a 180 turn, applied full throttle and headed straight for the intruders. Closing fast, my finger hovering over the firing button, I suddenly let out a sigh of relief. They were six Spitfires. More thankful than I thought possible, we carried on, eventually reaching Portreath safe and sound - almost. I landed first, and taxied right over to the control tower. Jumping out, I raced up the stairs so that I could help the new pilot on his approach. His first attempt was obviously no good, so I told him to go round again. His second was even worse, and he piled his plane into the grass beside the runway. I couldn't believe it after all we'd been through. Thankfully, with the help of the station fire crews, he and his navigator emerged unscathed.

TAILORS DUMMIES

In amongst the frequent Tsetse patrols we still did training flights, practising air to air and air to ground firing. One day I was approached by the CO of Portreath's ground defences. He wanted to give his troops some practice, and asked if I was prepared to do some dummy attacks. So there I was beating up and down the runways diving down on their gun emplacements. After one particularly low attack, I pulled back on the stick and was met by the most horrendous shaking. The stick was juddering so violently that I was barely able to keep hold of it. Fighting to stay in the air, I shouted at the tower that I was going to land immediately. Without completing a full circuit, I unceremoniously dumped the aircraft on the runway.

I had barely come to a stop when ground crew began swarming all over the place. The problem was found straight away. The top leading edge of the port radiator, which was between the fuselage and the engine, had fallen out! This had disturbed the airflow over the wing. It was this turbulence that had caused the juddering. Mildly irritated, I ordered that the missing part of my plane be found. Surprisingly, a keen eyed member of ground staff picked it up shortly after. On examination, it was quite clear that it had never been bolted in. With hindsight, I began to think how lucky I was that it had fallen out when it did. The aircraft had been on several ops, and it would have been unbearable, or even impossible, to have flown back from the Bay of Biscay with the stick dancing in such a manner! This wasn't the only example of such an error by factory staff. Soon after, one of my flight had a wing break up whilst in circuit over the airfield. This time it was found that someone had used glue that was past its best before date!

For some reason four of us were sent to Plymouth, setting off in a transport with a WAAF driver. My run of bad luck, mechanically speaking, continued. Half way into the journey we broke down. This time, however, someone must have been looking down on us for the van had packed up

During the original design stages it had been decided to use wooden construction for the Mosquito in an effort to ease the strain on Britain's hard pressed material suppliers. The lightweight result gave the aircraft an impressive top speed - generally above 310mph.

right outside a pub! Leaving the poor WAAF to sort out our transport, we all piled inside. Cornish pasties washed down by beer were certainly more welcome than a meeting at Group. Somehow the transport was repaired, and it was decided to return straight to Portreath. In Truro, I noticed a tailor's shop on the other side of the road. Needing a new service tie, I shouted at the driver to stop and hurried out. Unfortunately, the others followed in hot pursuit. Never before or since, have I tried to buy a tie whilst some merry companions were forming 'fours' with tailors dummies!

BLACK & WHITE STRIPES

No sooner had the Tsetse patrols become a way of life, than someone came up with another scheme for us to try. This time we were to co-operate with Wellingtons. We would escort the Wellington whilst it carried out a patrol for German Motor Torpedo Boats. As these tended to operate under the cover of darkness, a visual search would have been fruitless.

The River Odet with some German shipping.

To combat this the Wellingtons had been equipped with a new weapon - airborne radar. Once a 'plot' had been detected, the Wellington would swoop in, illuminating the target with a huge searchlight it had strapped to its nose. With the target conveniently spot-lighted it was up to the Mosquitos to finish the job! To get used to such a level of co-operation with the bigger bombers, we carried out a number of practices, attacking rocks in the moonlight, which the Wellington crew had illuminated.

On the 5th June 1944, we had an extremely busy day - and the planes did not even leave the ground. In a major effort both ground and flight crews combined their strength to carry out an extremely important task. Black and white stripes had to be applied to the wings and fuselage on every aircraft on the base by the end of the day - without exception. Now we knew that something big was in the offing! Briefings followed, and we found out that the stripes were intended to separate friend and foe and thereby assist in identification for the invasion forces.

The orders were explicit - anything in the air that did not carry these stripes would be the enemy. It was also pointed out that the Germans were now known to be flying aircraft captured from us, and might try and use these to infiltrate any possible landing area.

The 6th June 1944, D-Day, dawned wet and miserable. I noted in my logbook that the cloud cover was quite low, and that it rained at frequent intervals. I led the first patrol of the day, taking off just after dawn. It was a sobering thought to think that, whilst we were eating breakfast in the mess, soldiers from the largest seaborne invasion force ever mustered were battling their way ashore on the coast of Normandy. The idea of our patrols was to try and intercept any enemy aircraft that might try and reach the invasion area. We maintained a tiring, but constant, blanket of these patrols throughout the day.

Early in the evening we had a flap on. A reconnaissance patrol had reported sighting three German destroyers moving around the southern side of the Brest peninsula. Trying to stop these ships reaching the beachhead area, Group put together a large strike force. Eight of our Mosquitos were to provide cover for thirty-one Beaufighters from Nos. 144 and 404 Squadrons. As we flew south, we passed a convoy of six German minesweepers. They must surely have been unable to believe their luck as we completely ignored them. At all costs, we had to deal with the destroyers. Shortly after, we found the destroyers almost where we had expected to find them. Whilst we stayed as top cover, the Beaufighters swept in creating a never-ending barrage of cannon fire. One of the destroyers was left badly damaged and, chucking in the towel, all six retreated to the relative safety of Brest.

CLOSE CALL

On the 8th of June I led another patrol, and had a very nasty moment when I saw several single-engined aircraft. Naturally I was relieved when they turned out to be a patrol of Spitfires. The following afternoon I was in charge of a patrol of three Mosquitos that headed out over the Bay of Biscay. Things were quite routine until we saw an aircraft flying out from France. We gave chase and, catching it up discovered that it was another, lone, Mosquito. However it wasn't carrying any black and white stripes. Cries of "shoot it down" came over the R/T I got into a position on its tail and told Jimmy Orchard to flash the challenge letter of the day on his Aldis lamp. In reply, the Mosquito fired the wrong 2-star Very cartridge.

Whilst this aircraft has yet to be decorated with the black and white invasion stripes, they would have been placed around the fuselage and both wings.

Despite this, I felt that this was not a German and continued to give him another chance.

We were doing steep turns low over the sea. The crew of the other Mosquito fired another wrong set of identification cartridges. Then a frantic voice came over the R/T calling "don't shoot". The voice was definitely British! We escorted him back to Predannock, watched him land and then turned back for home at Portreath. When I entered the Op's room for the debriefing I was immediately asked why I had been firing on the CO of an intruder Squadron.

I told my Flight Sergeant to go and inspect my aircraft. He confirmed that not one of my guns had been fired - though this very nearly had not been the case. In retort I demanded to know what the devil the other Mosquito had been doing over France without the black and white identification stripes. Equally, why didn't he know the correct signal colours for the time and day?

The rather lame excuse was that the stripes made it easier for them to be seen whilst undertaking their intruder flights. Personally we all thought that he was lucky to be alive. It was only my indecision and gut reaction that had saved him for the others had all been in favour of opening fire!

ENEMY SHIPPING

As the Normandy Beachhead became more secure, the number of aircraft on each of the patrols was reduced to two. Despite this, the actual quantity of patrols was maintained, for example, I did two on the 13th and 15th June. On the 22nd, I did a lone reconnaissance flight from Brest south to the Gironde. The Germans must have taken to keeping their heads down, for it was another uneventful flight. On the return, I was flying low and fast over a very calm and glassy sea whilst looking straight into the evening sun. For some reason, I suddenly remembered my escapade over Lough Neagh. Deciding it would be prudent to put a little distance between the plane and the deck, I ignored the risk of German radar and started to climb. I could ill afford bent propellers this far from home!

With roughs seas this German convoy's problems go from bad to worse. The vessel nearest the camera is surrounded by spray thrown up by the cannon shells from the attacking Mosquito. This can be seen diving in from the left hand side.

By the end of June, we had started to carry 500lb bombs or depth charges in our bomb bays. Patrols were increased back to four aircraft, two with bombs, and two with depth charges. For good measure it was also common to have a Tsetse Mosquito included. I led one of these patrols down to Ouessant and into the mouth of Brest. There was low cloud and as you'd expect, we couldn't see a thing. Group instructed us that the fuses on the bombs were to be set at a three-second delay. Naturally we were all far from impressed. Our attacks were carried out fast and at low level, and when you dropped bombs like this, they were liable to bounce back off the water. If a three-second delay was set, it meant that you had a good chance that a bomb might bounce back up, and detonate near any aircraft that might be close behind.

The CO must have been on leave or away on a course as I took the opportunity to fly across to Thorney Island. This airfield was the home of No. 2 Group Squadrons, and they were renowned specialists at low level bombing. A three-second delay caused much raising of eyebrows. Their recommendation was to use 10 seconds - that way you had a greater chance that you would not be going round blasting your colleagues out of the sky! Back at Portreath I got straight on the phone, a call which resulted in an argument with the Senior Air Staff Officer of 19 Group. Afterwards I learnt that he was an Air Commodore! I must have had some effect, for only a few days later a new instruction appeared. All bomb fuses were to be set at 10 seconds!

THE DFC

On the 3rd July, two of us went on a reconnaissance flight of the Ile de Croix. On the return, I decided to alter the route, nipping in overland to cross the River Odet. This last minute change produced dividends, for there in front of us were two German 'M' class mine-sweepers. Shouting at my navigator that I would only be making one pass, he worked fast, and got some good photographs.

On our return these were shown to our Intelligence Officer, and our CO subsequently obtained permission for an attack to be made.

Flying cannon shells and exploding bombs envelope this German armed trawler. It is probably part of the escort for a small convoy which had tried to creep its way along from bay to bay in the hope of remaining undetected.

Next morning, preparations continued apace. Three of us were to attack overland from the Penmarche area. I was to follow the other two, remembering to leave at least ten seconds between us to avoid their bomb blasts. As they went into attack I circled with the engines throttled right back. I can remember passing low over a French farmer on a horse drawn cart with hay on it. I turned to follow, coming across a tree-lined river, flying at tree top height. At the same time the controls started going floppy - I was overdoing the slowing down. So, taking this as the right opportunity, I applied full throttle and dived in after the others. I was lucky - for there right in front of me broadside on was one of the minesweepers. I attacked with cannon, and released my bombs before racing on as low as I possibly could.

Captured in a fleeting moment by my navigator, Jimmy Orchard, the smoke in this picture marks the end of the Mosquito brought down in the raid on Penmarche. Crashing near Keranguyon Farm, both of the crew were killed, including the pilot, who was the CO of 248 Squadron.

I had seen one of the other Mosquitos diving on the other minesweeper. There'd been smoke, and as we raced out towards the sea we passed a tangled mess of burning wreckage. Over water once again, we found ourselves alone. Unable to raise the others on the RT, we turned for home. As we hit the Cornish Coast, we found low cloud covering the cliff tops. I turned west along the coast and after dashing between the shore and St. Michael's Mount, Jimmy produced a course that would steer us round Lands End back to Portreath. Nearer home, I heard another aircraft calling Portreath control tower. It was one of the other Mosquitos from the raid. Two of us had got back safely; the third had been brought down by anti aircraft fire from one of the minesweepers.

Its crew, our CO and his navigator, were killed. Despite this loss, our raid was classed as a success. Shortly after our attack, a PR spitfire took some photographs, showing one of the minesweepers awash. The second, badly damaged, was moored against a dry dock. I hadn't escaped untouched. Our Mosquito had been hit in the starboard engine. Shrapnel had hit the rocker cover, but luckily missed the important valve gear. Our port engine nacelle had also been damaged.

In the modest manner of Hal Randall, his diary entry for this attack is typically understated. For his part in this and other dangerous but successful attacks, Hal Randall was awarded the Distinguished Flying Cross. A copy of his citation gives a more clinical picture of the raid. Also in his diary there is a type written document produced in the 1960's. This describes the attack from a French perspective and reads as follows:

"It was about noon on the 4th July 1944 when three Mosquitos attacked the German ships at Penfoul Cove and the Kercreven dock. For more accuracy, the aircraft closed right in on their targets. As they skimmed over the masts of the enemy ships, they dropped their bombs.

"Anti aircraft guns were firing from Creach-Conarch Height and also from the ships. To this day, we have been unable to find out if Wing Commander Phillips's Mosquito was hit by flack. One witness claims that the aircraft hit the top of the mast of a German ship. The fact is that the plane only caught fire when she fell to the ground. The Mosquito crashed near the Keranguyon Farm and exploded.

"The pilot and navigator were ejected from the cockpit. The former was found near the crash site, whilst the latter fell 100 yards away in front of the doorstep of Mme Berrou's Farm.

"Both airmen were killed outright. Fragments and burning petrol from the aircraft fell on the farmhouse setting it alight. One of the aircraft's wheels crashed through the roof of the manger.

"Two farm workers, Yves Glemarec and a young girl named Yvonne Laurent had been watching the attack from the top of a hedgerow. When they saw the Mosquito coming straight for them they quickly took shelter behind the hedgerow. Yves Glemarec had time to tell Mme Berrou to take cover. She hit the ground behind an old wall, which was blown over by the explosion, but was unhurt.

"In the crash, the two farm workers were covered in burning petrol. Their clothes caught fire. Yves Glemarec was badly wounded but he survived. Yvonne Laurent died twelve hours later. A third civilian casualty was Mme

Capp, who was wounded in the arm. The injury was so bad that her arm had to be amputated. The Germans ordered the two British airmen were to be left where they fell. It was two days before an Officer appeared, and gave the instruction that they be buried."

CRASH LANDING 4

A remarkable series of photographs that follows the fate of F/L Stanley (Baby) Nunn's, Mosquito damaged during an attack on German shipping. As the armed trawler is smothered by the bomb blasts it puts up a spirited defence (above left).

Hit by the anti-aircraft fire one of the Mosquitos banks away, smoke pouring from its left hand engine (circled, above right). Escorted for home, and with one engine out, the damaged plane crosses (bottom left) first the Bay of Biscay, and then back over British soil (bottom right).

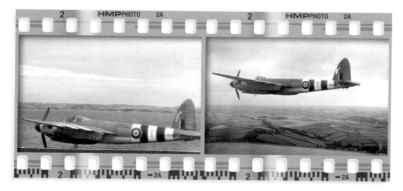

Landing first, I rushed round and was able to capture the aircraft executing a perfect belly landing. Hitting the runway its slides past other parked aircraft (above) trailing sparks and dust, before finally coming to an almost gracious halt right in front of the camera (below).

On the 10th July, we left on an early morning raid down to the Gironde. As we passed between the Ile de Yeu and Belle Ile we spotted two coasters accompanied by two armed escorts. They were following a course of 330 degrees. Trying to report the siting we found that our WT was not working so we returned as fast as we could to Portreath. We left again at midday; a force made up of ten of our Mosquitos and six from No.235 Squadron. We found the German ships slightly closer to St Nazarie. My bombs overshot but I did better with my cannon fire.

The progress of this raid is best described by the amazing set of photographs taken from Hal Randall's Mosquito.

ROVER PATROL

Another view of the business end of a Mosquito, taken from another Squadron photograph.

On the 27th July I returned from nine days leave and found that the Squadron was operating another new form of patrol. These were the Rover Patrols. These operations were basically a slight adaptation to the work that we had been doing in the days after D-Day and, as before, involved Mosquitos from the Tsetse flights. On a Rover you could, within reason, patrol any route you desired. The target - any enemy shipping that you encountered. It mattered not whether it was an armed trawler, a minesweeper or a fully-fledged convoy of destroyers. If it wandered into your path, then you had the opportunity to engage it!

On this first Rover since my leave, I was in charge of six Mosquitos from our Squadron, along with two from the Tsetse flight. We hadn't been out over the Bay of Biscay for long when an opportunity presented itself - a convoy of six ships. As ever, throttles were opened wide, and we started to climb allowing us to dive down on the target. Preparing myself, I armed my guns. This involved flipping up the cover over the arming switch before pressing it down. This had been an automatic reaction the moment that the ships had come into view. As I tipped my Mosquito into a dive, with the rest of the patrol banking round to follow, I gave a quick squirt on the firing button to test my guns. Silence. Cursing, I tried the switch again, but still my guns remained steadfastly silent! I couldn't believe it!

I was now faced with a dilemma. Should I continue to press home my attack without being able to fire a thing? A charging Mosquito with four cannons and four machine guns blazing away was formidable and tended to make the gunners on the ships think very seriously about their safety. However, a large two-engined aircraft that was defenceless would provide them with a juicy target to concentrate on! The simple alternative was to break away. Deciding on the sensible option, I broke, telling the others to press on with the attack.

They pressed home and had some success. The Tsetse's made several telling hits, though two of our Mosquitos had to limp home on one engine. No sooner had I landed than, once again, I had the ground crew find the source of yet another fault. It transpired that the cover on the firing switch had somehow become distorted, so that it prevented the firing button from making a complete contact when depressed.

MIST

Eager to make up for the lack of success on my first Rover, the next day I led another operation to the Gironde. Again there were eight of us, three Mosquitoes from No 248 Squadron, three from 235, and the ubiquitous pair of Tsetses. Making sure, I tested my guns as soon as we were safely out over the English Channel. They worked! Despite the fact I was now capable of making an attack, we saw no shipping. All we managed to achieve for our efforts was a lot of inbound anti aircraft fire as we flew past the Ile de Re at low level.

On the 2nd August we repeated the same operation, though this time heading for the Ile de Croix. It was as if I was never intended to lead a successful Rover, for as we rounded the Brest Peninsula, we hit several belts of heavy rain. Flying low over the sea these squalls looked like a solid wall. Although we were not flying in close formation, we had no difficulty in maintaining station as we found it quite easy to look out to

Located during a successful Rover patrol, this armed trawler fell victim as cannon shells rip across the water towards it. There can be no doubt that the boat was hit as the trail of erupting water continues on the other side.

the sides of these belts of rain. After about three or four of these showers, we approached another, which turned out to be quite different. This was sea mist, and presented a less desirable obstacle, to say the least! Once inside, you become totally dependent on your instruments. Not only were you no longer able to see out of the sides, but your grasp with the horizon completely disappeared. Opening up my engines and managing to keep level with the help of my artificial horizon, I gave the order to climb, telling the others that under no circumstances were they to bang into me! Climbing through a 180-degree turn we eventually emerged above the mist. Having been scattered by the mist we all made our own way back to Portreath. It was a sad moment when it was finally accepted that only seven of us had returned. No trace of one of the Mosquitos has ever been found. Exactly what happened will never be known. It is likely that the pilot was too slow in turning to his instruments to get him out of the mist.

Two days later, two of us were sent on a different mission. Our task was to patrol the area around the Channel Islands and the shipping lanes to St. Malo. Intelligence had been receiving reports that the Germans might be evacuating the Islands. Staying at arms length, for the Islands had been turned into veritable flak fortresses, we patrolled for several hours. Not one ship was encountered. Returning to base, we reported that if the Germans were evacuating, it was going to be a painfully slow and drawn out affair.

ONE-UPMANSHIP

Despite the fact that it was August, mist was still going to plague me. On the 6th, I flew one of the Mosquitos back to De Havillands, and collected another that was to be brought back to Portreath. Spending a few hours at Blackbush, it was late afternoon before I began to approach Portreath. On arrival, surprise, surprise, a dense sea mist lay across most of the airfield. A break appeared in the mist revealing half of the runway. I did a very quick circuit before bouncing down onto the small piece of exposed runway. Even before the end of my landing run, I was back in the mist. It was with some difficulty, and at a snail's pace, that I taxied my way across to the dispersals.

Sighing with relief, I climbed down from the cockpit. The ground crew told me that some flying boat types were visiting the station, and were being dined in the mess. It transpired that they heard me arrive and land, and because the mess was enveloped in the sea mist they were somewhat mystified. Sensing the moment for a bit of one-upmanship, one of my colleagues stated, in a rather matter of fact manner, that we often landed in such dense mists! To say they were impressed would be a slight under statement. Eager to maintain the impression, I swaggered into the mess hall to join them, conveniently forgetting the break in the mist through which I had just landed!

Six days later, on the 12th, another Rover was sent to the Gironde. This raid though was one with a difference. A total of twenty-one aircraft were to be involved, from both 248 and 235 Squadrons. Six of these aircraft were to carry bombs. We all flew directly to a point south of the mouth of the Gironde, turned east heading overland until we reached the river before turning one more round towards the mouth of the River. There were seven ships at anchor and all twenty-one aircraft dived in for the

Once again German shipping, in the form of the ubiquitous armed trawlers, is the target in the pictures of this attack. Bombs burst (above), while cannon fire straddles the vessel below. If you magnify this picture it is possible to see a lone gunner steadfastly remaining at his post on the bow - not a pleasant proposition with all that cannon fire flying around!

attack. With that number of aircraft and ships there was tracer flying left, right and centre. I can tell you that it was with much relief that I swept over my target and headed out to sea. Sadly, two aircraft were lost. Both were brought down by flack and ditched in the sea. In both cases the crews were lost.

The day after the raid Group had us repeat the same operation. Perhaps because it was the thirteenth, we didn't get very far. One of the pilots had knocked his radio transmission open. Consequently he had blanked out everyone else's RT so we couldn't tell him what had happened. Equally, his transmissions would have enabled the Germans to hear us coming! As a result the raid Commander instructed us to turn back.

LAST MISSION

This was my last mission - attacking German shipping in the mouth of the Gironde. This Mosquito lines up his attack, bomb doors open and machine guns and cannon blazing.

On the 14th August 1944, I flew my last operational sortie. Keeping in the pattern of our recent missions, it was to be a large formation. Twenty-four aircraft were gathered for the raid, and realizing it was to be my last trip,

Bombs gone, the Mosquito pulls up (above). It is at this point that he is most vulnerable to anti-aircraft fire, with his underneath completely exposed. The strikes of his cannon fire can clearly be seen on both the water and the boat. I follow close behind to make my attack. The attack was reported in the daily papers (below).

I was put in charge. Conditions couldn't have been better. We took off at 1900hrs on a truly gorgeous summer's evening. We flew direct to a point just south of Lake Carcans, before turning inland over the fir forests. We were flying so low that it was even possible to smell the pine fragrance. It seemed a shame to spoil such a pleasant evening by doing what we had to do.

Hitting the river, we turned towards the mouth. At the same time our targets came into view. Sitting obediently at anchor was a destroyer, two 2000-tonners and a number of flak ships. I went for the big one and attacked the destroyer. I used up all the cannon before breaking away over the southern side of the river. Weaving hard, I was a bit put out, as

110

some unfriendly devil seemed to be firing tracer at me every so often. A couple of moments later, I realized where it was coming from. In my panic I was still clutching the firing trigger. Every time I pulled back on the stick, I was also pulling on the trigger. Hence the tracer was coming from my own .303 guns. What a relief!

In some ways, this was a sad end to my operational career. We lost a total of four aircraft, three from No. 248 Squadron and one from No.235. Despite these losses, possibly as a result of the sheer size of the attack, someone at Group took the decision to release the details to the press. Imagine my surprise a couple of days later, when I saw my name in print. In the meantime, I had completed 200 operational hours. From now on I could only fly non-operationally. To start with, I helped train some of the new crews for our squadron before, on the 26th September, I was posted to the RAF Staff College at Bulstrode Park.

WEDNESDAY, AUGUST 16, 1944

acks — "STAR" NEWS REEL — MOSQUITO ATTACK NEW IN

Bombs from low-flying Mosquitos straddling an enemy vessel off Royan, France, when RAF Coastal Command planes flew up the mouth of the Gironde and attacked enemy minesweepers and trawlers.

This picture of the operation, my last, was printed in the Daily Star. It is worth comparing this officially released image to the one I had taken on the opposite page.

POSTSCRIPT

Having completed operational duties, Hal continued flying duties with the RAF until the war's end. With peace, Hal continued on with his RAF career, including two years in Egypt. It was not until 1965 that he finally hung up his flying hat and retired. Even to this day Hal cannot forget the operations that he undertook during his time in Coastal Command. He has always borne the memory of the effects that these missions would have had. Here, though, he has never distinguished between his colleagues, the enemy, or the occupied. Indeed he has since been back to the Penmarche area, the scene of the attack described on page 98. This visit was made at the official invitation of the French and, as their guest of honour, Hal was asked to help dedicate a memorial to some lost aircrew.

Listening to Hal I have no doubt that this trip had a profound effect on him. It helped him come to terms with the losses inflicted by the flights over occupied France. During this visit the French treated Hal with nothing but admiration and respect. It was made clear to him, especially by the families of the Frenchmen mentioned in the text, that they did not blame him or any of his colleagues for the losses that the French population endured during the war. Yves Glemarec, who was badly burnt in the attack on page 98, even presented Hal with a bottle of his home made Calvados. Whilst it was with deep sadness that such losses were accepted, the French people told Hal that they understood the necessity of the attacks that the Allied aviators carried out. Such losses and damage are seen as a regrettable and unavoidable part of the struggle to free France.

Combrit, France, 30th June 1944. Laying a wreath at the graves of P/O Tonge and F/S Rigby, who were both killed in action on the 30th June 1944.